Follow the
Cow Path Home

Daryl –

Happy memories!

Chuck Hackenmiller
9-8-12

Follow the
Cow Path Home

Memories and verse of mid 20th-century Iowa

Chuck Hackenmiller

ISBN: 978-0-9831961-9-8

Published and printed in the United States of America by The Write Place. Cover and interior design by Alexis Thomas, The Write Place. For more information, please contact:

The Write Place
709 Main Street, Suite 2
Pella, Iowa 50219
www.thewriteplace.biz

Copies of this book may be ordered from The Write Place online at www.thewriteplace.biz/bookplace.

Dedication

This book is dedicated to my parents, Rudy (who died in 1996) and Marcella Hackenmiller. The two supplied deep roots that nurtured the growth of their ten children (three sons, seven daughters), and built fond memories of the family farm. Thanks, too, to my wife, Mary Ann, and our three grown children for their encouragement to write this book.

Contents

Forward

So much has been written about agriculture in the early 1900s: many memoirs mentioning the use of the muscle-bound, hard-working horses used in farm operations, the rural, rugged, self-sustaining lifestyles that thrived and didn't allow anyone to go hungry.

Eventually with the coming of new decades, the sunrise of automation yielded to new implements that helped improve efficiency and production in farming operations.

This book details farming life in the era between the late 1950s and 1960s when modernized changes in farm practices loomed on the horizon, before tillable acreages grew by leaps and bounds and prior to the family farm numbers decreasing in rapid proportions. This is the era when rubber wheels replaced the steel wheels on tractors and wagons, when use of the moldboard plow was considered practical and not anti-conservation like it is today, when chickens roamed freely around the farmyard and hogs couldn't get enough mud in their dirt hog lot, when home-cooked food beat "eating out" menus any day of the week.

While much of the writing is derived from personal life experiences living on a farm in northeast Iowa just south of the Iowa-Minnesota border, many who lived on similar farms during this generation will likely find themselves, and their lifestyles, on these pages.

The setting proved to be a good indicator of what farming was like in most of Iowa during this era when, thanks to the always-abuzz telephone party lines spreading across long stretches of gravel roads above the barbed wire fences, neighbors enjoyed being downright neighborly and were forever willing to lend each other a helping hand.

It's a time that is still fresh in the memories of many, yet still considered something that was lost in an ever-changing countryside. The pace was seemingly a bit slower, when families could talk about their day's experiences while all gathered around the kitchen dining table to feast on a home-cooked meal.

Permit me then to invite you to join me at the table for a literary feast, if you will. Digest some of these memories and then relax in that easy chair or sofa to relish the meal. Close your eyes and visualize, or take a well-earned nap.

In doing so, my hope is to enlighten, refresh some memories, and share some of my stories and poetic verses.

My goal, then, is to "lead you onto that cow path, and bring you home."

Follow the Cow Path Home

CHAPTER 1

Walking the walk

Along, leisurely walk through alfalfa-laden pastures has been a common thread that ties together many a farm boy or girl.

Here's how I picture the memory today.

It's about four in the afternoon on a lazy summer day. The evening milking chores are a couple hours away. The feedlot near the barn is void of bovines. All of the cattle are in the north pasture, grazing on the fresh green grass that sprouted from the previous nights' rains. It's time to bring the cows home.

The walk down the tree-lined lane leading to the farm pasture begins. Rats. The cows are grazing in the corner of the field that is the furthest away from the barnyard. Wouldn't you know it? Particularly on the day that my legs are weary from a full day of pitching manure from BOTH the chicken house and hog shed.

I grab a fallen branch found in a nearby grove of trees and fashion it into a walking stick, then move on toward the northwest, angling toward the setting sun, making sure to keep my distance from the charged electric fencing wire.

At an early age, you HAD to know west from east, north from south. Why? Because someday you would be called upon by Dad to plow the west field, or cultivate the corn on the south fifty acres. There's nothing worse than misinterpreting directions, tearing up the wrong field, burying some crops along the way. Yep, you'd tend to get your ears boxed for that.

Dad made it easy to remember. "The sun always rises in the east and sets in the west. The Minnesota border is to the north, the opposite is the south. So learn those directions," he would say. So I continue to head toward the setting sun.

I can smell the clover from our nearby hay field. Won't be long and it will be time again for baling the second cutting. I trudge ahead, use my stick and swing it like a baseball bat at the prickly tall thistles looming in my path, knocking the noxious weed flat on the first swat.

Oops. Need to watch where I step in this pasture. My fairly new high-top work shoes, purchased from Stacyville's only shoe store, sure don't take a shine to fresh cow pie.

My pace quickens, knowing that it's going to be a long walk to get the cows home for the evening milking chores. Supper will be waiting for me when I get back to the farmyard, and I've worked up a feed-bunk appetite.

At about the halfway point of my walk in the pasture, one cow looks up at me and then bows its head low to the ground for another chew. No use hurrying. They seem to know me as well as I know them. They've got time to get a few more chews, because I'm still a few good paces away. The cows' tails flick incessantly at the flies that land on their rumps.

Now as I draw nearer to the cows, one by one their heads bob up. The move is on.

Instinctively they know it's time to head home, and their radar kicks in to find the oft-traveled, dirt-bare cow path visible on the pasture ground. First one cow finds it, another follows, and soon all the cows move single file, looking downward upon the well-worn, winding path as they move slowly to the barnyard—their expansive udders swaying left and right and looking mighty full for the night's milking.

Cows rarely stray from that winding cow path in reaching their destination.

Once arriving at the barnyard, the Holstein herd heads for the nearby barn's water tank to satisfy their huge thirst. When the last cow gulps its drink and the water level is low, several small catfish inside the water tank—lightweights from a recent fishing trip—come up and splash with reckless abandon at the snouts of the lingering cows. The fish are likely wondering where that full tank of water disappeared to so fast. More water trickles from the hydrant to the tank, and the water supply is replenished for the next time the cows require a refreshing drink.

You know, without that cow path, just think of what chaos would abound in rounding up the cattle for the night milking chores. It's amazing that the cows sought out the path rather than making a disorganized dash to all corners of the pasture. But then again, each knew where her path would lead her.

No matter how far they wander from that path to seek even greener pastures, they instinctively know how to get back on it and find their way home.

In metaphoric comparison, I figure it is similar to the familiar gravel roads we traveled over and over again when going to nearby towns or other farms. You know you'll eventually get there, if you stay on course.

I compare it to those oft-traveled highways and byways we find ourselves navigating during our journey through ordinary life.

Many sometimes stray from what appears to be their destined path, but there's always that increasing urge to return to that safe corridor, or comfort zone, that will take them home—if only for a few seconds, a moment, hour, or day to reminisce—and to quench that thirst for the memories of days gone by.

What Iowa farm boy or girl doesn't have some strong memories of growing up in the wide-open countryside?

Memories lead us home. In my situation, it was a small Mitchell County farmstead in northern Iowa that was the subject of some pleasant reflections. But I'm probably not alone in my thinking. There are others likely having those "I remember when" stories gathered in their mind's treasure chest, shared during a holiday meal among family and friends.

To sum it up is a poem I wrote, published several years ago in an Iowa publication, which I titled "Iowa's Glory." The contest subject mat-

ter required by the book publisher was how we would summarize our
life in Iowa. I chose to write about living in the rural areas.

Iowa's Glory

What about this ebony soil-rich land
that inspires growth from seeds of imagination,
fostering ingenuity, mixing it to the flavor
of a fertile agricultural empire
that we call Iowa.

Here, where time can pass so fleetingly,
the world stops for a neighborly chat,
indulging in generous spiels about
nothing consequential, dabbling in idle
conversation about the weather.

Find Iowa in the fields' clear ponds
reflecting puffy clouds on a summer day.
Follow the sweeping sky-high corn rows,
walk on the cows' dirt-trodden path
leading to a place where hearts call home.

And the spirited Eastern Goldfinch will soar
above the mighty oaks, happy as a lark,
grasping a keen sense that this is where it belongs.
The same wind that rustles through its colorful feathers,
whispers over the plains, leaving no doubt about Iowa's glory.

CHAPTER 2
Living off 140 acres

Our dairy farm resembled many smaller 1950 through 1970 Midwestern farms that dotted the rural landscape. It wasn't huge in respect to total acres, but it had variety in land usage and new and old farm structures. The primary, most important building on the farm, of course, was either the family dwelling—if you perceived that notion from the mother's perspective—or the barn, from the father's perspective.

Perhaps a typical farmhouse may have looked like ours did: a two-story dwelling with the parents' bedroom on a main floor that also included a kitchen; dining room dressed with a huge table surrounded by benches or chairs; living room that had a piano and if lucky a television for entertainment; one bathroom; study area where there was a desk for school homework or space reserved for accounting and paperwork for the farm; and a front porch to hang the winter coats or offer storage for perishable grocery items. The upper level had several boys' and girls' bedrooms and closets, plus an attic.

We were fortunate to have a concrete-floor basement, often musty but important nonetheless for storing fresh garden produce on open shelving. There, too, was the old, heavy, immovable freezer that stored home-butchered chickens and other meats, baked bread, cookies, and cakes made from scratch. An old ice box contained a few homemade brews of dandelion wine and numerous other knickknacks. Other neighbors may have had only dirt floors in their basements, used only for seed potatoes, some food storage, or for shelter in a severe storm.

Our often-used basement also contained a makeshift shower, something Dad rigged to wash our bodies free of the thick-layered, caked-on dirt, grain dust, and manure we accumulated on ourselves after a long day of work. Because there was just one bathroom, which meant one mirror-attached vanity and one toilet and one bathtub in the entire house, taking turns and setting time limits were critical to keeping the peace among parents and siblings in the home.

In winter, the coziest, warmest spot to stand upon in the whole four-bedroom house was the eight-square-foot grate that covered our oil furnace that heated the home. It was on the main floor, in the dining room area. If you looked down into the darkness below the grate, you could barely see the flames burning within the furnace, once powered with coal. With the dawn of new heating technology and natural gas

This two-story dwelling was home to Rudy and Marcella Hackenmiller and their ten children. In later years, after the farm was sold, a fire destroyed the house.

conversions, the oil furnace was retired to the rafters of the corn crib, where it provided shelter for pigeons seeking relief from the winter wrath.

Initially, warm air from the oil furnace rose to all corners of the house. In those days, there were no heat ducts that brought the forced warm air to the bedrooms upstairs. So the children with sleeping quarters on the second floor used layer upon layer of extra-heavy blankets and old quilts to keep the chill away during the long winter nights.

Imagine waking up in the subzero cold mornings, peeking out the ice-glazed upstairs windows before stepping onto a frigid carpet-less floor, then alas—realizing that everyone else had beaten you to the punch searching for that little corner of warmth of the downstairs furnace grate.

So the trick was to get up before anyone else. You snoozed, you lost your space. We stood on that furnace grate, barefoot, until the grate marks made indentations on the bottom of the feet, or until mother came calling from the kitchen with the hot, steamy kettle of oatmeal in her hands. If it wasn't oatmeal or hot breakfast to lure us from the grate, it was a couple slices of hot, toasted homemade bread, colored lightly, buttered thick, and sprinkled with sugar and cinnamon.

The heat and humidity of the summer required diplomacy among the upstairs children as we took turns sleeping beside an open window, inhaling the breezes that filtered through the screens. Some nights, the wind was non-existent, and so went the fortunes of a good night's sleep, with pillowcases sopping wet by morning's call.

In our family house, the space was divided among twelve—parents and ten children. At one time a grandparent lived with us. He and his wife had farmed the same land and raised a family there. That was in an era when most of the stored horse harnesses and yokes, steel-wheeled wagons, and other antique farm equipment were put to good use. When Grandma died, Grandpa remained on after my folks married and took over operations. Grandpa died on that same farm, doing what he loved best—working the land.

Logically, the kitchen was the busiest place in the house because it seemed hunger never subsided with our clan. Someone was always opening the refrigerator door or buttering fresh bread sliced from a loaf that came straight from the oven. Obviously, only the home's bathroom, with its stacked copies of the Wallace's Farmer or Successful Farming, might have been more occupied. Outhouses were still prevalent then in the early 60s, but not as common since the age of indoor plumbing and porcelain toilets made their debuts.

Mother was always cooking, baking, or canning. Preparing three meals a day (we called it breakfast, dinner, and supper while some call it breakfast, lunch, and dinner) happened to be a monumental task. Throw in the fact that Mondays were set aside for laundry and baking and Saturdays for house cleaning, and it was overtime and more for the girls in the family.

Fortunately there were seven girls in my family who could help carry on these tasks, not to say that the boys couldn't contribute now and then with the housework by straightening out their bedrooms or dresser drawers and keeping their designated clothes piles in somewhat tidy order. That being said, the girls also helped with outdoor chores and took turns behind the tractor wheel.

But we boys couldn't bake a lick, and we were usually doing more of the "trackin' in the mud and manure" than the cleaning—so we stayed out of the way of the cooking, the brooms, and the dish rags, and we were steered more toward taking care of the livestock or planting and harvesting the primary crops of hay, oats, corn, and soybeans.

Our barn wasn't the typically pictured huge, red, wooden structure with white trim, an icon one might connect to the dairy industry and seen in many picturesque magazines. It was a drab gray color and appeared much smaller in stature, with the roof and sides covered in corrugated tin. Inside, it held up to thirty wooden stanchions on each side of the barn walls, separated by the manure gutters and concrete aisle.

There were a few calf pens tucked away in the corner, and unfortunately for us, there were still plenty of places for the Holstein cows to roam when they didn't want to move into their respective stanchions at milking time.

On one side, facing south, the barn had a double door, hinged at both the top and bottom. Through that open top door, I gazed to the south at the country scenery as far as the eye could see and took in the sweet-smelling aroma of fresh cut hay in a nearby alfalfa field. From there, one could see the neighbor's silos or a late evening rainbow stretching above the cornfield. What a place it was for leaning on, and for daydreaming.

The hayloft above the milking floor usually didn't have a lot of room to wiggle for work or for child's play, since the bales were stacked tight and full to the roof after the hay harvest. But once the bale count dwindled and we could see the loft floor, we'd have the opportunity to have some fun swinging from the rafters, jumping from here to there. We had to be careful not to fall through the loft's hay chutes placed strategically over the hay mangers or feed alleys below.

A crevice within the barn's interior woodwork was a haven for families of kittens. Cats were everywhere on the farm, as were generations of dogs. Many of the farm families had generations of pets to remember—some of them performing double duty as work dogs that brought the cows home from the pasture or as tomcats that killed rats that liked to hide in the piles of ear corn.

The hog shed was among the newer buildings on our farm. Dad would buy feeder pigs and we'd raise them through different stages for market or for butchering. Often we'd butcher one or two and keep the meat in the basement freezer to last throughout the long Iowa winter. On butchering day, the meat saw ran continuously as relatives also assisted in the packaging of the various cuts. There would be evenings when casings would be filled with sausage meat—luscious for those great tasting egg and sausage meals. The fat would be melted down to lard and even the brains, tongue, and pigs' feet were harvested for human consumption.

We'd also hold back a few sows, and inside two converted brooder houses packed with wood and steel crates we'd have a small-scale farrowing operation. Many a late night was spent under the brilliance of the heat lamps and warmth of the straw as we watched the birthing process, making sure the sow wouldn't lie upon its litter.

Each spring we'd get baby chicks, sometimes arriving through the mail. The chicks would arrive in boxes punched with breathing holes, and the peeping sounds would get louder as the boxes were handled. The brooder house, when not used for farrowing, would house the tiny chicks that were warmed with several heat lamps hung near the waterers and the small feeding pans.

Eventually the chicks would leave the "cute" stage, as well as the brooder house, and grow into these rowdy roosters or pullets. The roosters enjoyed ruling the roost on our farm, giving chase quite often to taunting, then frightened cousins who visited from the city. Some roosters were just plain mean. They had a way of making us and our city cousins humble. We wouldn't feel so invincible when running up against a smaller two-legged creature.

But it was the city cousins that got the last laugh as they returned to their homes with the butchered roosters that they could cook for their Sunday meals.

The hens, once they were allowed to roam the grounds, found the apple tree branches to their liking at night. It wasn't until they were past the pullet stage, when they laid their eggs in the most unlikely places throughout the farm, that we began hunting and climbing trees for the roosting hens and getting them back inside the larger chicken house, where the egg gathering was so much more simplified. Still, we'd suffer from scratched arms or pecked hands just to battle a stubborn hen for her eggs because she refused to leave the comfort of a straw-field nest in the henhouse.

Two buildings on the farm basically held the harvested corn and oats.

The oats went into a two-story granary on the first floor level. In the upper level of the granary, remnants of farm tools used in the past were stored, such as horse harnesses and bridles, an old plow, or a hand-cranking corn sheller.

The granary was a place of storage for the oat crop. The corn crib in the background was one of the newer buildings on the Hackenmiller farm.

In late fall, the harvested ear corn went into a two-sided, roofed wooden crib. The corn crib also had a dirt alley right down the middle of it, where the combine, tractors, and "too old and not-for-highway-travel" truck could be parked.

All had to be cleared out of that corn crib when it came time for shelling the ear corn and grinding it out for livestock feed. Once the wagons were filled with the shelled corn, these wagonloads were also parked inside the crib. Above, across the rafters of the corn crib, were long two-inch by eight-inch boards that spanned the space above the corn-filled wagons. Dad walked on these boards to adjust the elevator chute when filling the crib bins with the ear corn during the fall harvest.

However, when the parents were gone, we young ones used the boards as launching pads to jump into the wagons of shelled corn about ten feet below us, not thinking of the consequences if we happened to miss the corn piles and land on the dirt floor below. Didn't really know if our parents would appreciate what we were doing, or if we'd ever get in trouble for it if they did see us playing our game. We only hoped they remembered being adventurous as kids, too.

The cobs left over from the shelled corn were crushed by the hammer mill and used as floor or nest bedding in the chicken houses. The cobs weren't just for the outhouses anymore.

Another busy place on the farm was Dad's workshop, where he had his old welder that he used to piece together lots of broken objects for projects such as the sickles that broke on the oat binder or hay mower, or to mend a part from the combine, or for fun when he put on his eye shield and used his welding rods to repair an old bicycle. As kids we slipped on that oversized protective eye shield and stared into the sun, hoping perhaps to see a solar eclipse now and then.

The workshop was my favorite place to be on a rainy day, often just looking for some old tool treasures that were stashed underneath the thick wooden shelves; pounding some nails in the work bench; dragging out Dad's Prince Albert tobacco tin and the rolled paper that was inside the pigeon-holed shelves that also carried spare nuts and bolts, screws, nails, and other odd items; scooping out the old, pot-bellied stove inside the workshop, investigating its contents that carried trash that never made it to the burn barrel; sawing some scrap wood using the custom-made sawhorses; sharpening my pocket knife on the work bench grinder; and looking for baby kittens from mother cats who found the workshop walls a nice shelter to give birth to four or more at a time.

Attached to the workshop were the garage for the cars and also the milk house, where the milkman stopped daily to load and unload milk cans from the icy cold cooler. He transported the milk cans to the town's creamery. The milkman also left butter and a milk check for our family. The hydrant inside the milk house had the coldest water I had ever tasted.

Our soil was rich and fertile. Dad strongly believed in crop rotation, and he never farmed completely from fencerow to fencerow. He used the moldboard plow in the fall and assigned his sons the responsibility of disking, harrowing, and other fieldwork.

A creek ran through the northeast and east sectors of the farm. The waterway was a popular place to watch tadpoles and to scare up some pheasants now and then.

Corn was planted and harvested either as silage blown into the two tall silos (some area farmers had three or more silos) or as picked ear corn. Later on, corn was harvested with combines, replacing the one- or two-row pickers, which put the traveling corn sheller man and his equipment out of business.

Oats stood tall and golden until a wooden wheel shoved the cut stem and grain onto the rolling canvasses of the binder, which spit the cutting into neat windrows. After a day or so of drying, a combine made its way through the windrowed piles.

Soybeans began making a consistent showing in our fields in the 1970s and beyond, working their way into the crop rotation.

Eventually, the old barn couldn't hold all the hay bales we harvested in a year, so a new hay shed was built for second and third cuttings of hay. After the hay shed was built and the farm operation grew, along came a couple more steel bins to store more grain.

All these structures served a useful purpose. No farm building space was unoccupied. Even the run-down buildings were used for storage or for a horse stall.

The lay of the land?

How does one stake ownership to the land that's served generations before us? My father and his father, and ancestors before them, had borrowed the land to sustain their families and raise whatever income the farmstead offered. There never was an abundance of earnings, but we never went hungry.

The land and its crops were always at the mercy of Mother Nature. Ourselves and neighboring farmers had been wiped out a few times by wind and hail. We had all seen a good share of hail or early frost damage crop insurance adjustors.

But the land gave many a decent living and a way of life that could never be taken for granted.

Much of our land remained planted into corn, even when the high-market-priced soybeans entered the picture. In the west parcel was a pond area that never felt the tickle of a plow or disk. For many years it was set-aside land, or diverted acres. The only things we harvested off the parcel were a lot of fun and some bruises from the spills we took as kids when ice-skating on the ankle-deep pond situated on the conserved acres.

A grove of trees surrounded the acreage where our buildings and homes set. One summer night, a twister ripped through the farm place, carving a "V" shape through the tops of the trees in the farm's grove. It came very close to the house, knocking down a tree that stood near the basement of the home.

That same night, I remember someone running into the house to alert us that bad weather was arriving and that we needed to take cover. All of the family went into the house's basement. Mother brought her Rosary and we all huddled together in a corner, away from the windows, while she led us in prayer. Her prayers must have made a strong shield, as there were limbs down around the house, but no buildings had fallen.

As kids we'd scurry to the nearby creek bed and reach in and find tadpoles, or just walk in to soak our toes on those hot, muggy days, which were common on the land and the farm where I grew up. At nights you could hear the chirping of the crickets and the toads croaking as they made their way down the small stream in the creek bed.

Someone told us that if we kept the tadpoles in jars long enough, they would turn into frogs. Problem was, we should never have used our mother's good canning jars to try and prove that theory. Boy, did we ever get in trouble for that stupid move.

Never remove an empty jar from the house during canning season. Ever. It's a cardinal sin.

CHAPTER 3

The two-a-days

"Ker-chup, ker-chup, ker-chup, ker-chup."

Sound like a bird chirping outside an open window, or in the grove of trees?

Perhaps the noise could be mistaken for that. Actually, it was a certain sound that could be heard mornings and nights inside the barn.

Most dairy farmers who remembered the years that succeeded the "milking cows by hand" phase can identify the sound of the "ker-chup"—the Surge brand pulsators chugging back and forth while the suction cups, attached to the lid of the milk bucket, stayed solid on the cow's teats.

The suction cups slipped on the cow's teats, hugging tight and allowing no air leaks. Each pulse of the milk bucket, which hung on the metal bar from a leather strap wrapped around the back and belly of the cow, meant milk was flowing freely from the teats into the bucket—or at some farm dairy operations, into a pipeline that flowed to a large, sanitized tank in a separate room in the barn.

When pushing the front and back of the udder, you knew when the cow had given all the milk it could. I would reach for the air tap above the cow's stanchion, shut off the suction, and pull off the hose attached to the air tap. I would then lug the milk bucket to the milk cans in another area of the barn. Some cows gave a whole bucketful. Some, drying out, covered only the bottom. The milk cups would flap against the metal of the Surge bucket.

I would lift up the cups on the lid of the milk bucket to release all the remaining air inside it. As I raised the cups, there was an exhaling sound. I would raise the bucket lid and dump the milk into a strainer sitting atop the milk can. A circular pad inside the strainer separated the impurities from the milk as it slowly drained into the numbered milk cans, one of several ready and waiting to be filled during that morning or evening milk session.

Then it was on to the next cow, udders and teats washed ahead of time and ready for the milk bucket and suction cups. The strap was taken off the previously milked cow and placed on the cow that was next in line. Milking wasn't over until the last belly strap had been hung on the large spike pounded into the barn wall. When the milk buckets were rinsed and hung on the wall, the cats were always given a helping of cream poured from the strainer into an old pie tin.

That's a scene one might have repeated over and over again with the small twenty- to fifty-cow dairy operations in the 50s, 60s, or 70s, repeated twice daily. Today, some milking operations are producing milk twenty-four hours a day.

Night milking usually started right after the evening meal. We'd finish eating around six p.m., let our meal settle, and before we could relax too much, Dad would leave the house and go straight to the milk house to load the cans on his homemade cart that was pulled a few hundred feet to the barn. In the barn were about twenty-seven stanchions, empty and waiting for the cows that had gathered in the barnyard after a day in the pasture.

In the winter, the cows stayed inside the barn for all but a few hours, let out for the removal of manure from the stalls and gutters and to allow the herd to gulp water from the outside water tank. While they drank, we would spread straw for their overnight bedding.

To coax the cows back into the barn, we'd throw some silage and some crushed corn onto the feed aisle in front of the stanchions. It was also a reward for the cow to find the right stanchion.

It's amazing how most cows knew exactly which stanchion was

theirs. But there were times when a cow couldn't instinctively remember. To be disoriented and be off a stanchion or two would cause confusion and chaos among the other cows entering the barn. It turned out to be an unpleasant task to correct the cows and get them back in their respective places for the milking chores that morning or night.

We had seen cows lost in the feed aisles, jump inside the calf pens, and lost in the parlor, all because some cow misjudged its stall space. When the cow inside a wrong stanchion saw all that feed in front of it, it lost all sense of direction. That usually didn't get the milking sessions off to a good start, as our tempers flared. I can still see my dad getting red-faced, saying a few choice words to the lost cows.

Once things settled down, and the cattle were moved to where they were supposed to be, we reached for the six milking straps and put them on the bellies of the cows. On came the old radio with the faded dials as we hoped to hear maybe a Minnesota Twins baseball game, local high school or college sports broadcasts, some good soothing music (which seemed to relax the cows), or Lowell Thomas and the CBS national news.

A flip of a switch turned on the motor for the pump that distributed the air suction piped to the taps above the stanchion. We had four Surge milk buckets going at the same time—Dad, my brothers, or I had the duties of manning the buckets. Dad normally handled the milking of the new heifers, which were experiencing the whole process for the first time and were "none too thrilled."

The troublesome heifers attempted to kick the milk buckets into the next county, which raised my dad's ire. While we were eager to add another to the milking herd, heifers were sometimes really a pain.

The bloodied milk from a cow that had just calved was fed to its weaned young one, which was penned inside a small fenced-in area within the barn's parlor. The calf didn't take to the milk pail too easily at first. Sometimes, bottles had to be used. Eventually, the calf joined the other calves in the pens and eventually grew to become part of the herd or was taken to market.

Once the fresh milk from the mother cleared, it was good enough to run through the strainer and into the cans. Each cow wore a numbered tag so that Dad could keep a record of the cow's milk production, health issues, and breeding record. He started a new page for each new heifer.

While we waited for the cows' udders to empty, I would dig the jackknife from my pocket and begin whittling at a piece of scrap wood or a stick I had picked up earlier and brought into the barn. Sometimes while waiting I just leaned on the side of the cow's rump, elbows holding up my head, and I daydreamed. I woke up rather startled when the cow raised its tail and filled the manure gutter behind it.

After we finished the milking, it was up to the loft to throw down some hay through the chutes—fodder for the cows to munch on over-night. The hay was spread in the feed aisle during the winter months, and in the summer the bales were placed in feed bunks outside the barnyard.

That being done, the full milk cans were hoisted on the cart and moved back into the milk house into the multiple-can milk cooler where icy cold water would run continuously over the cans to prevent milk spoilage.

Morning milking began early for Dad, as he awakened at 5:30 a.m. to begin the milking chores. He often ended up doing the whole morning milking by himself, at least from August to May, because my brothers and I had to get ready for our long bus ride to school.

There's a whole lot more associated with the milking chores that extended beyond the evening and morning routines. Every day, with the cows inside the barn or out grazing in the pasture, we took the time to clean out the often soupy manure from the barn's gutters by pitchfork or shovel, throwing the animal waste into the manure spreader or tractor loader. The calf pens also had to be cleaned out and fresh straw bedding reapplied.

The manure spreader was taken to the fields, and the rear beaters would fling the waste onto the farm's fertile soil, where it served as a nutrient for next year's crop. That was a tedious job and one that Mom fretted about often because we'd have to wear those same lovely smelling barn-cleaning clothes to the dinner and supper table. But it never seemed to ruin our, or anyone else's, appetite. Mom always made us wash up squeaky clean in a sink, or usually at the basement faucet.

I envied our neighbors who had those "automated" gutter augers that dumped the inside manure outside into the spreader with less human effort. It made that boring chore go much faster.

The women in the family weren't exempted from the milking operation. Their task included washing the milk buckets wherever steamy hot water was available, often in the basement of the house. They cleaned the suction cups and the strainer on a daily basis with a strong disinfectant—a requirement from the local creamery staff who consistently tested the milk's quality.

Between milkings, usually around midmorning for us, the milkman arrived. The milkman had several stops up and down the road at other dairy farms before reaching ours. I was always amazed at the strength of the milkman who seemed to lift the full milk cans two at a time with a single swoop into the square box of his truck. His time there was short— maybe five or ten minutes, long enough to fill our order for butter and drop off our replacement milk cans, new milk strainer pads, and the all-important milk check. If he collected six full cans, he left six empty cans, all bearing the same number painted red on each can.

Once the milkman hit all the other dairy farms on his route, he pulled into the nearby town's creamery. He unloaded the cargo of milk cans onto a conveyor, and, through newer automation, the milk was dumped into a holding tank. Each can was then thoroughly sprayed and sanitized, ready to be dropped off the next day at the farm place.

One aspect of being a dairy farmer—it didn't leave much time to do anything else on evenings or mornings other than the milking or feeding of the dairy herd. There was no straying from the twice-a-day, seven-day-a-week milking duties. There was no rest on Sunday. Sure, it was a day of obligation, for church AND for milking cows.

It wasn't healthy for the cow, or the family's finances, to skip a milking or two. The cow could suffer from mastitis, which kept the cow from milk production until she was fully healed. So visits to relatives or neighbors would be planned in the afternoons or at times after the milking—never during the milking hours.

After the summer evening milking, it was the end of a long, hard day of work. We could kick back and do whatever we wanted while there was still daylight—possibly play in a ball game with the neighbors or catch up with a hobby or two. Sometimes I'd lie on the storm cellar doors and catch the sunset, or count the stars in the sky until it was time to go inside, ready for all to turn off the lights and go to sleep.

In the winter after an evening of milking the cows, we could come into the house and warm ourselves near the furnace, watch some black and white television, maybe catching the end of Bonanza, or cozy up with a good book.

I can remember going to my grandmother's house in the summer, after milking, when there was that extra daylight. We'd have fun in her yard and gather underneath her weeping willow tree, swinging from the low branches. We'd catch fireflies.

Some evenings after milking we would all hop in the station wagon and while plenty of daylight was available, our parents would take us on a drive through the country as they looked at the neighbors' crops. Somehow, we'd always end up in a town nearby and there would be this place that sold great malts or ice cream cones. That was our treat for a day of good, hard labor.

Back home again, to bed, and to get our rest for another busy day.

The cows rested too, and were at peace in their own straw-laden stalls while chewing their cuds.

CHAPTER 4

Those knotted bales

It was about early summer when the smell of sweet clover drifted over the family farm, and soon after it was time to prepare for that first cutting of hay. It was my favorite of harvest times.

This was well before the big roll balers of today that now leave round bundles of hay or straw dotting the rural landscape. These were bales of fresh hay popped out the rear of the International 45 baler chute, neatly tied by twine, in a tight rectangular shape. Those bales were stacked on endless convoys of hayracks and eventually unloaded into the barns or hay sheds by bale fork, elevator, or manual tossing by a strong lad or two.

The first piece of equipment used in the hay harvest, be it the first, second, or third cutting, was the mower. Since storage space was at a minimum for all our farm implements, we parked the mower, over the winter months and throughout the spring, in a grove of trees on the farm place. Once needed, the mower was bolted to the drawbar of the Farmall H and the power takeoff shaft of the mower was attached to the tractor. The motion of the power takeoff moved the well-oiled triangular sickles back and forth on the long sickle bar, raised up and down with a lever pushed by the mighty legs of the tractor operator.

To ensure a clean cut of the hay, it was important that each sickle on the bar be sharp. Some badly nicked sickles had to be removed and new ones inserted on the sickle bar, kept in place by rivets. Into the workshop all the dull sickles would go, and each had a destiny with the workshop grinder. The sparks would cascade down to Dad's feet as the grinder met the steel.

Once all was in place, the first cutting commenced, as long as the weather forecast didn't predict rain for the next few days. Climate was important and made a strong case for a trusted weather prognosticator. There was nothing worse than hay spoiling in wet fields or stressing out our arms and the baler with heavy, moist bales.

Hay field acreages were rarely huge back then, unless the farmer had a gigantic cattle operation and decided to put up both bales and chopped hay. Our hay fields averaged about fourteen to twenty acres. Round and round we'd go with the hay mower, starting on the outside and working our way to the middle of the field.

We shared our baling implements and harvest of labor with the neighbors, who had large families of their own. Before starting the hay harvest, we'd go to the town's primary implement dealer and purchase bales of twine. While there, I'd listen to the adults talk about the markets, crop yields, and gossip. It was the same place we'd bring our tractors in for repair, and buy our new sickle blades, tractor mufflers, and parts for

Everyone was involved in the hay harvest, even the neighbors and cousins, at the Hackenmiller farm.

most any other farm implement we had in operation at home. Sometimes, however, we saved because there were spare parts on some of the old machinery discarded throughout the farm.

When it came down to hay harvest duties, there was someone who drove the side rake that would whip the downed hay into neat rows. Those rows of green always made a unique pattern on the rural landscape. This was an easy job, but it was boring ... so tedious. It was better than cultivating corn, though, when one could almost nod off while on the tractor seat.

With wide-open hay fields, dozing while driving wouldn't be as damaging, unless you didn't wake up until too late and found yourself driving through a neighbor's fence. But I've heard tales of farmers, or their sons or daughters, getting the case of heavy eyelids while cultivating and eventually wiping out a row or two of young corn or soybean plants.

Someone had the job of driving the tractor that pulled the baler. This job was usually designated to a younger male or female who had some raw tractor-driving skills. I did it for a share, as did my younger brothers and sisters and the neighbor's children. It was our initiation into the harvesting season.

The trick was to keep the back tractor wheel close to the windrow so that the baler augers behind could sweep up the hay and keep it moving through the chute of the baler.

"Ker-chunk! Ker-chunk," sounded the baler as its tines swept the hay toward an auger that shoved it into a chute, where the hay was bunched together, tied by the automated knotter, and counted, then pushed up the chute toward the hayrack. At the end of the day, the small counter attached to the side of the baler was the true indicator of a day's work. Counting was important, as it helped in calculating yield numbers and was instrumental in determining if there was adequate space available in the lofts for all those bales.

Another skill necessary for driving the baler was to not release the tractor clutch with sudden quickness. The rack attached to the rear of the baler would also jump, upsetting the neatly stacked bales of hay. Down the bales would come upon the wagon stacker, or the hay bales would roll off the sides of the rack.

The person stacking on the hayrack had dual responsibilities. It was a skilled position, because the bales on the hayrack had to be placed on the wagon just right so that dips or gopher holes in the fields wouldn't force the bales to tumble. Bales had to be stacked at least five high for a full load, although neighbor boys boasted that they could stack hayracks eight high or more if needed. Some used hooks to dig into the bales as they came out the baler's chute. Others used their hands, covered with gloves to fend off the blisters, to get the stacking done in a smooth motion before the next bale came out of the chute.

The stacker also had to be the baler mechanic. Sometimes the machine would take in too much hay and would have to be unclogged. Or the knotting mechanism would have to be recalibrated, or the bale of twine had to be replenished. Or the bales would start getting heavier as the day progressed, once the heavy dew and air of nighttime arrived, and handles on the baler chute had to be twirled to tighten or loosen the twine and lighten the load.

As one hayrack was filled, another worker brought an empty rack and took the full rack of bales back to the barnyard. The bales were placed on a bale fork, or an elevator, which brought the hay through an open door to the loft. Two or three workers, including the farm owner, would be inside the barn or hay shed to stack the bales step by step as high as the loft's rafters.

The best memory of hay-baling day was the mid-afternoon break, when out to the field, riding an empty returning hayrack, came the whole hay-baling crew. With the group would be a pitcher of ice-cold lemonade and a plate of cookies, brownies, lemon bars, or other dessert fresh from Mom's kitchen. We took a half-hour break and just relaxed under the shade of the fully loaded hayrack, visiting a while before getting on with the task at hand.

The most rewarding part of baling hay or straw was when the last load was taken from the final windrow and the tractor, baler, and load of hay came home all at once. You'd feel the evening's cool breeze on your weary, sweaty back as you returned by gravel road from the field driveway to the house. The sunburn you had earlier was now engrained, becoming a deep tan.

Barns were built in all shapes and sizes. When it was the neighbor's turn to bale, he'd have the same number helping out, only he'd have someone also driving his Farmall B in the farm yard. The feisty little tractor pulled a rope that helped lift a fork full of six to eight bales to a overhanging pulley. Once the bales reached the pulley, they moved laterally into the barn. Someone inside the loft would yell "pull," and the person sticking the fork on the hayrack would tug at another rope, and the bales would drop from the fork down to the barn's hayloft floor.

During the evening milk session, the fresh hay smell filled our senses. At the end of the day, the cows would relish the fresh hay, thrown down from the hayloft, once the last milk machine was hung on the hook.

The haying process would be repeated for a second crop, and sometimes a third or fourth crop, all depending on what the weather gave us. At times, once the hayfields were harvested, we'd be allowed to have a neighborhood baseball game where the windrows had been. It might have been a bit rough to field ground balls on the lumpy ground, but we didn't care. Sometimes we'd use the lawn mower to make base paths and a batter's box. The back of the hayrack, covered by a canvass, would serve as the catcher.

The baler was put away until later in the summer, when it was time to bale straw once the oats were harvested. The straw was used as bedding for the livestock and placed in hay sheds, livestock buildings, and available space in the barn. Straw bales were easier to handle—much lighter, and the process went much faster than that first crop of hay.

All in all, you slept pretty good on those nights of hay and straw baling, knowing that a good day's work was done.

Hay Baling Time

The hayfield is mowed. Alfalfa smells fresh.
Dad lifts the first cutting, checks for dew below.
Satisfied the hay is dry, the churning
side rake piles the hay into patterned rows.

Forget about the trip to town
to watch the Independence Day parade.
Today the ball team will be one player short
because today there's hay to be made.

Ker-chunk. Ker-chunk. The baler inhales the hay,
not leaving a single morsel on the ground behind.
The young stacker, shirtless and sunburned,
piles the wagon high—hoping the twine binds.

And when the wagons are unloaded and piled
high inside the barn—sometimes ten bales high—
the heat infiltrates the humid hay loft and we're anxious
for the end of hay-baling, or a cool breeze, to draw nigh.

The sun begins to sink and
the hay bales get heavier and tough.
But the day won't end until the
hayfield's been declared clean enough.

When the day is done and the tired crew
brushes off of them the hay chaff to the ground,
we're blessed with a reminder of today's work
as the fragrance of sweet clover abounds.

The rain can fall now.
The hay crop is in.
Until that second crop grows tall
and it's baling time again.

A Good Sweat

In the muggy hayloft, heat is grueling.
Sweat streams down the chin.
Bales jump off the hayfork
and loose chaff sticks to the skin.

Detasseling corn under a beating sun,
perspiration stings the eyes
and penetrates hidden cuts on the forehead from corn leaves—
bringing on painful cries.

Under a hazy blue sky
bean walkers struggled to endure
the humid heavy climate
that makes working conditions poor.

In the livestock sheds
that often need cleaning out,
sweat makes the pitchfork handle slippery
as pesky flies are all about.

The taste of sweat is salty
as it trickles on the lips.
Shirts become wet throughout
and stick annoyingly to the hip.

However, when the long hot day ends
and cool breezes follow a setting sun,
there's nothing more fulfilling than knowing
another hard day's work is done.

The Smell of Rain

It's been a long dry spell.
Disappointments make it hard to cope.
Dark clouds tease, raising broken spirits
only to pass, offering an empty hope.

Then comes a distant thunder.
Once again anxiety stirs.
Will this weather front yield some moisture
before more drought hardship occurs?

Suddenly, a brisk cool breeze blows.
Scents from the country fill the senses.
The humidity will soon be lifting
as nurturing of the land commences.

Before the anticipated storm draws near
and sprinkles fall upon the flesh—
appreciate, partake of the sensation
to inhale the air clean and fresh.

All of the parched earth benefits
From the drenching that it gains.
But another most satisfying feeling
is to absorb the splendor before the rains.

CHAPTER 5

Those itchy oats

I don't believe there was any older piece of machinery on our farm than the rust-coated, dilapidated binder that cut down the oat crop year after year.

It was one piece of machinery that stood inside the machinery shed corner collecting spider webs during the other three seasons of the year. It was parked near the pull-type combine that, too, was tucked away from everything else.

The canvasses needed for the binder were stored in the rafters above the dirt floor of the old machine shed. Before oat cutting commenced, we'd pull down the canvas and check for parts that needed patching. This was a necessity because our free-range chickens roosted on the shed's rafters, and mice that miraculously escaped the farm cats sometimes found ways to reach onto the canvas and gnaw through its tough material.

Once the tractor pulled the oat binder out of the shed, the binder was checked in detail for wear and to see if any parts were missing or needed to be replaced. The equipment was already plenty old—but it was well taken care of, I thought, by Dad and Grandfather. A squirt or more from a tube of grease on all the farm equipment worked wonders. No farm was without grease guns, and many farms purchased their grease by the barrel or in tubes.

We looked at the sickle bar in the front of the binder and checked for loose or worn sickles. Sharp sickles would cut down the belly-high standing oats like falling dominoes. We looked at the patched wooden wheel that pushed the cut oats onto the canvas of the binder—I often referred to it as the Ferris wheel—to see if it would stand up to the task for one more year. The canvass moved along on rollers, which coaxed the cut oats to another canvas and then out of the side of the binder, into windrows.

The rusty binder had an old cast-iron seat attached to the rear, placed there specifically for someone to work the iron levers back and forth. The levers raised or lowered the head of the binder so that it could cut down as much of the standing oats as possible, increase the crop yields, and leave straw behind. In some areas, such as along wet patches, the oats didn't grow as tall and the head of the binder required lowering. A comfortable seat? Not really. It wasn't cushioned like the red and white seat of the tractor that was pulling it along.

Once the oats were on the windrow and the binder put away for another year, one of the biggest pieces of equipment on the farm, the combine, was moved out of the machinery shed and parked in the driveway under the shade of a stand of pine trees. There, it was readied for the oat harvest.

The many different sizes of belts on the combine had to be checked and tightened once more, and it was also vital to give the equipment a thorough grease job before taking it out into the fields.

Over the years, we had a variety of different combines to work the fields. My parents had talked often about the old horse-drawn binders, the remnants hidden in the stands of trees or groves or storage sheds, the equipment eventually taken apart for scrap iron. I can remember no thresher on our farm while I was a child—although I'm sure there had been well before I came along.

Recollections take me back to a McCormick combine that didn't come with a power take-off shaft. We had to crank-start an engine attached to the combine, and that engine would power the belts, the grain and straw separators, the gears, and all the bells and whistles of the horseless wonder. We went to a newer combine later in life—one that my dad had picked up on a bid at a neighboring farm auction. This orange-colored Allis Chalmers combine came equipped with a PTO shaft that ran all the mechanical parts of the implement. We eventually graduated to an older-model International self-propelled combine.

Dad always drove the combine. Like a baler, the rolling tines picked up the windrows. Once the oats were inside the implement, the grain was separated from the straw. The oats were channeled inside a hopper on the combine, while the straw fell softly from the back of the combine to the ground below. It was amazing to see how the oats could be shook and separated from the straw with such little waste.

My duties and that of my brothers included bringing out the empty wagons and bringing back the full load of oats to be piled inside the granary.

There was nothing as enjoyable as a wagon ride to and from the fields, as this photo from the 1960s suggests.

The John Deere-green grain elevator chute dropped the oats into a pile in the back of the granary building. The grain elevator's spout hovered through a narrow window in the granary, and it dropped the oats onto the top and bottom floors of the building. It was always a test of skill to back the head of the grain elevator through the narrow window of the granary—someone had to do the "backing" while another stood away cranking at the gears that heightened or lowered the spout of the PTO-powered elevator. It was important to stay away from the overhead wires.

Once the adjustments were made to the elevator, the first load of oats came through as the grain flowed from the hydraulic wagon's end-gate into the elevator's auger. This task wasn't always the most pleasant, because the chaff from the oats happened to be very itchy. Chaff was plentiful, particularly when you had to enter the granary to shovel the oat piles around and distribute the grain evenly throughout the floors of the building.

Load after load, it would be like that. On our small farm, the value of oats was deemed tremendous. Oats were used in a mix with the shelled corn for hog and chicken feed, and sometimes crushed through the hammer mill all by itself for dairy feed. Some of the oat crop was harvested by chopper and blown into the silos, also used as feed for the cattle.

At the end of the day when the oat crop was harvested, our exposed skin and clothes were blackened, from head to toe, from the dust and chaff brought on by the oat harvest. We'd do our evening chores and then head to the house. The showers were extremely busy at the house on those nights. Water in the tubs and basins was pitch black after we washed up.

Once the oats were in the granary, it was time to bale the golden straw. Straw served many purposes on our farm. It was used for stuffing the hen's nests in the chicken house, and for bedding for cattle and the other livestock during the cold winter months. The straw was stored in whatever buildings were available—the hog house, some lingering spaces in the hayloft.

The stacked straw in the buildings also sometimes proved to be a haven for mice, seeking warmth from the wrath of winter, and for wasps and hornets that found straw irresistible for shelter. Those were some of the pests we had to deal with on occasion.

The dawning of self-propelled combines sped up the harvesting process immensely—for oats as well as corn and soybeans. Today the heads of these monsters cover a much wider swath through the golden field of oats. Matter of fact, you don't seem to see a lot of oats being grown these days.

Primarily, it's just corn and soybeans, from fencerow to fencerow.

The two-wheel oat seeder itself was unique. In the spring when planting commenced, the seed oats were poured into a funnel-like hopper on wheels, and as the oats got to the bottom of the funnel, two whirling augers would fling the seed onto the prepared ground. There was a mix of alfalfa with the seed, so that once the oats were harvested, it became the next year's hay crop or pasture.

An oats field at its prime, ready for harvest, presented a golden view for those that would pass by it while they drove by on the country road. And it also presented itself as one of several golden memories that stayed with this farm boy.

I can remember one summer day in particular, when a passing storm drenched the farm. The sun emerged, and a glorious rainbow stretched into the fields, passing over the bright yellow field of oats and providing the most vivid, colorful view that couldn't have been painted on any canvas.

All that itching from the oat harvest, the times scrubbing like crazy to get out all the dust from the hair, well, it was just all part of the harvest cycle.

Morning's Curtain Call

Act One began in darkness, well
before the birds all started to sing,
setting the stage for a grand entrance
of a brilliant sunrise from the wing.

The backdrop was that of trees, grass
sparkling from the morning dew.
On the set were bright red barns, houses
and cattle waking to a day fresh and new.

Lights inside buildings flickered on
and life started stirring from within.
A tractor engine broke the country silence
as the hardy task of chores begins.

Chickens in the hen house cackled
and the farm scene came more alive.
Hungry dogs and cats begged to be fed,
happy to see daybreak finally arrive.

The sun's rays closed in on the garden,
the warmth helped the flowers bloom.
Nothing matched the spectacular view
staged right in nature's living room.

What a magnificent show it was
for those who hadn't observed until now.
Nature, it's time to answer the curtain call.
You deserve to take a bow.

The Tinker

If things didn't break, or go awry,
if every machine would purr on the first try.
If we could build by only following directions,
or repair faucet leaks just by tightening connections.

If simple old ways would stay the same,
present and future going along with the game.
But no, times change as each day comes along
and nothing is invincible, or forever strong.

From welding a pitchfork to making a bell ring,
we need a tinker who can do so many things.
Things like fixing a lawn mower, making cars run
should be thought of by that person as nothing but fun.

The tinker's memory still clings to the past.
He can revive yesterday's machinery with knowledge that's vast.
The tinker remembers old tools of the trade,
the parts and pieces of how things are made.

The tinker shrugs off financial success,
but works at his best, not settling for less.
His rewards are not measured in gigantic profit sums,
but instead in listening to an old engine hum.

Since the world's not perfect, material gets old,
A reliable tinker is tough to mold.
We don't realize how precious that tinker can be
until we lose a treasure nobody can repair—but he.

CHAPTER 6

The five-buckle bonanza

There they were in the town's lone clothing store, standing tall in the small front window display.

The treasure? Five-buckle boots.

These items were as important for farm footwear as the high top Red Wing steel-toed work shoes, because they protected the shoes from the winter slosh, the mud.

And manure.

Yep, it happens. Manure, no matter how disliked, is a major part of farm life for those lucky enough to raise cattle, hogs, chickens, or other livestock. If you wore the brand-spanking new five-buckle boots to school, you made sure there was some sort of identification etched inside, such as a name or a phone number. Losing a pair of five-buckle boots was like losing a billfold—they gave so much identity in themselves.

The five-buckle boots became farm household fixtures. In Iowa, they were a farmer's prized possessions, ranking right up there with the bib coveralls and the winter cap with the pull-down earflaps.

The black-colored, shiny boots were washed often, and they were mourned when a hole could no longer be patched.

It was a signal of adulthood when dads took their sons or daughters to the nearest shoe store to purchase their first five-buckle boots.

First thing noticed when opening the box containing the new boots was the poignant smell of new rubber. On the bottom of the boot, emblazoned in white, was the boot size. Mine was 13 for the longest time.

I had to wear one or two sizes more than my regular shoe size to make my foot fit. It was important each boot fit well. They had to be worn again and again, and had to last, for a long time. Trying them on in the store was essential.

Once the shoes were inside the boots, the buckles were tested, starting from the bottom and working on to the top. You wanted to make sure that the boot fit tight enough around the top so that it would cuff around the pants leg, but loose enough to slide off or on without tugging and tugging and tearing the heel of the boot or snapping off a buckle. Nobody liked to have manure dripping inside their boots and onto their insulated socks.

During the first few weeks, while the new boots were being broke in, any spot of manure was washed off with focused attention. Standing at the water hydrant and spraying the boots with the hose only took a few seconds. Then the boots were left outside to dry, ready for use the next day.

And the next day, the next day, and the next day. Golly, you almost lived in those boots. If you could wear them to church and school, you would—but only if your parents consented.

There was obviously always a need for five-buckle tall boots. You were constantly in the muck and manure. Protecting the work shoes and the pant legs from the odors had been high priority to mothers who didn't want everything tracked into the house. The mothers didn't want to follow their husbands or sons around the house, spraying each room with the sweet-smelling lilac aroma that came from an aerosol can.

What can you say about manure?

Pitching manure into the spreader was a daily chore, like it or not. Cows needed fresh bedding often, because dirty udders were not fun to deal with when milking chores commenced. After backing the John Deere manure spreader into the barn entry, we'd grab all available pitchforks and pile the manure high into the spreader.

The spreader would then be pulled out to the fields by our Farmall H tractor, where the manure moved by apron to the beaters in the back end of the spreader. Manure served as valuable nutrients to the tillable soil. When the farm fields were impassable because of soft, wet soil, or because of snowdrifts, the manure was piled high somewhere near the barnyard and then moved out in the spring to the fields prior to planting.

Some days it would take only thirty minutes to clean the gutters. But on days when the calf pens also had to be cleaned out, it would be a full-morning affair.

Saturdays were usually reserved for pitching manure out of the hog pens. Hog manure, according to our mother, was the worst smelling because it lingered longer. Many times we couldn't step inside the house because of the odor. We'd have to take off our clothes in the basement, where some freshly washed clothes would be waiting for us. We'd have to use the old basement shower before stepping into the kitchen, living rooms, or bedrooms of the house.

The hardest chore on the farm, I believe, was cleaning out the chicken house. The manure was tough to break up with the pitchfork, and it was a time-consuming, sticky task. Once it was finished, we'd grind up piles of corn cobs and use that as a base for the bedding.

Sometimes, if your smelling senses were working right, you would know what type of livestock was been raised on neighboring farms just by sitting next to the farmer's son on the school bus. All had their distinctive odors. The dairy farmer, the hog farmer, and the chicken farmer had odors that stayed with them. City kids thought it wasn't right for anyone to smell the way we did. Farm kids knew, however, that the livestock smell was "the smell of money."

I can remember a small poem someone recited to me during a bus ride. It came from the boy who I sat next to on the school bus—a dairy farmer. My friend smelled like milking equipment sanitizer.

"I saw a birdie in the sky. It dropped some bird poop in my eye. I didn't worry. I didn't cry. But I'm ever so glad that cows don't fly," he said.

Truthfully, there's nothing more satisfying than getting a livestock pen floor clean of manure and spreading fresh straw on that same floor for bedding, then watching the livestock kick up their heels in their fresh, clean environment. It's backbreaking work—all this cleaning out calf pens or the hen house. But it helped make the day fly by.

My dad used manure pitching as a tool for punishment, too. Anytime we did something immeasurably wrong, like staying out too late the night before, he'd have the calf pen chore circled on his mental time clock to be done for that day, without breaks except to come inside the house for dinner or supper.

Many boys earned money by pitching manure. It was part of their condition to gaining an allowance.

That money was enough to buy more five-buckle boots to replace the older boots that either decomposed, lost buckles, or allowed moisture that seeped inside the shoes. Some wore their boots in the winter months to school on days when snow fell and the feet had to stay dry.

Sadly, as useful as these boots were, they never lasted forever.

Then we had to buy new five-buckle work boots, another treasure in the minds of a working farm boy (or girl).

That First Chore

My nervousness was apparent.
I'd never ask Dad this before.
But it was time to take more responsibility.
I wanted to be assigned a chore.

"I want to grind the corn,
and feed the livestock on the farm.
I'd enjoy helping with the milking
and carry bushel baskets in my arms."

Dad said: "Sure, it's time for you to
accept the role of a farmer's son,
to learn the ropes, get to know
how jobs on the farm should be done."

So he let me feed the chickens, gather eggs—
menial tasks I took in stride.
Each day the chores had to be done.
But one day I let it slide.

That day, feeders were empty, nests full of eggs
when Dad checked on my job.
I shattered his confidence and when
he spoke in disappointment, my heart throbbed.

"Responsibility should not be an act,
one that is taken so lightly.
Do that in life, you'll go no place.
Remember that when doing your chores nightly."

Eventually I regained his trust.
What a tremendous lesson to be learned.
No matter how boring, difficult the task,
responsibility, like trust, should be earned.

CHAPTER 7

Finding God, peace

When growing up, the nearby small rural town I came to know as a young lad didn't have a large water tower as its tallest landmark. Instead, a keen eye from afar would have seen the spiral steeple of Visitation Church sticking out like a sharpened pencil pointing to the skyline. The bells of the church could be heard around the countryside each day during the noon hour, alerting those outside to come inside the house for some nourishment.

The population within and surrounding the community was comprised primarily of Catholics. The brick, steep-roofed, accommodating church provided the town's foundation of faith and the center of activity for many years—a place where people gathered to give thanks and alms to God, to socialize, and to plan parish events. You could see the strong foothold of a revered faith through weekly worship, goodwill activities, or the participation of the church parishioners and "circles" with their families on any given Sunday.

One of the biggest events celebrated by those who attended the church came in the fall—the parish bazaar. Rural and city circles of women helped prepare the food to feed hundreds, while the men worked various shifts at fund-raising booths such as the popular bingo stand or paddle wheel. The day's highlights, beside the filling parish dinner, were the benefit auction and the raffles. Top prizes always included a quarter or half of beef or pork, along with merchant donations. Sure enough,

A church steeple near Meyer, Iowa, appears beyond this field.

there were also beautiful quilts and homemade items to buy, provided by talented and dedicated women of the parish.

Those from the city and country came together that one bazaar Sunday each year to bond in their faith with a spirit of teamwork.

Still, one might say that our rural environment outside of town was one of the biggest churches in the world. Granted, it didn't have crosses, statues, or rows of pews throughout the rolling acres. But you could see signs of God during every daily endeavor.

"Where?" one may ask.

One didn't need to look very far. Then again, sometimes you didn't have to seek at all—it just appeared before your very eyes.

There were beautiful sunrises to see, glorious sunsets to fathom, all within clear view in the fields and yards of the rural homesteads. On the days that were busy and the family put in a hard day's work, sitting back to see the breathtaking glow of a color-changing sun as it went down below the western horizon was a fitting climax.

As the twilight entered, and you sat on the open, wide-cushioned

Farmall tractor seat, getting in that last round of corn cultivating or bringing home that last load of harvested ear corn, you could smell the rich earth as it mingled with the evening's dew-laden air. There was beauty in a seed that, once planted and nurtured, poked out of the acres and acres of farm ground and formed straight green rows as far as the eye could see.

In the winter, a coat of fresh snow made every tree on the farm, even the tall elms, a magnificently decorated Christmas tree. In the fall, colorful leaves waved to us while still firmly attached to the branches, then dropped harmlessly to the ground when the stems lost grips on nature.

On a cloudless night, you could drop your back to the ground and leisurely stare at the dark heavens to count the stars, undimmed by city lights, and you could point to the Big Dipper, Little Dipper, and occasionally catch a glimpse of a falling star or an airplane skimming across the sky. The still of the night was broken only by the chirp of crickets, croaking of toads near the creek, a hooting owl nesting in one of the nearby trees, the whisper of the breeze brushing through the tall grass.

In the heat of the summer, there were fireflies to catch and the sound of the water gurgling through the creek bed after a downpour. After the rain, there was usually a rainbow that captivated the attention. A haze sometimes hovered above the ground, going no higher than the treetops, and a deer bounced out of the fence line and continued bounding into a nearby wooded patch of ground.

Once in a great while, a huge jackrabbit or a pheasant made the heartbeat flutter as it popped out when you least expected it when walking the fields. All God's creatures had a place in life, a time in life, and a purpose in life.

And there was beauty, too, in birth and rejuvenation. The hand of God was present when you found kittens cuddled together in a crevice inside the barn, snuggling and waiting for their mother to provide some nurturing; the miracle of life in the palm of your hand while holding a baby chick for a second or two before placing it back under the heat lamp; or gazing at the litter of grunting piglets nursing under the warmth of the mother sow as they jostled for their meal ticket. There was precious joy when watching puppies in a playful mood, and seeing the lambs and foals get strength in their legs and jump wildly throughout their dwellings.

Watching the birthing process, a miracle in itself, was humbling. I've watched cows give birth, both in the fields and in the barn. From the cow's womb, first to come out was the calf's front hooves, followed closely by the calf's head. The rest of the calf slid out from the cow and landed near fresh straw. The cow immediately began cleaning its young, and soon, the calf's wobbly legs made their way to fresh milk from its mother's udder.

Fathers on the farm would tell you that the true beauty of nature was seeing a pile of surplus ear corn outside of the corn crib, indicating that it was another bumper crop, or seeing the price of their commodity rise to profitable levels. He'd say tasting that first raindrop on the lips, after a long dry spell, was most rewarding, and that having the equipment void of breakdown through the harvest seasons was such a blessing.

Mothers on the farm might tell you that they thanked God for the bountiful gardens, for a functioning sewing machine, for good laying hens and egg prices, for dry breezy days to hang clothes outside on the line, for neighborly, caring friends, and for a time to sneak away from it all with a walk down the farm lane or along the country road.

Christmas lights that were placed on or around the house looked so serene against the snowy landscape when seen from the barn. Yet, from the house looking to the barn, the lights from the windows of the barn, in the darkened winter hours, were just as comforting and peaceful, providing a surreal farm setting.

The church in the distance, too, was not forgotten. On Sundays, it provided a spark of warmth and renewal and instilled the drive to begin another week full of opportunities, promise, and more. The lights of the church, as we drove from the country into the parish parking lot, were so inviting—particularly on Christmas Eve when the nativity scenes seemed impressive and the glow of the candles inside warmed the kindred spirits like a winter wrap, or during the Easter season when incense drifted into the church balcony.

There is no better place than to sense the presence of God, than in the solitude of the church itself and in the church of the land, the places that we were most comfortable worshipping in because we found Him so near to us.

The Little Things

The father called all to the table
and said: "Let us bow our heads.
Let us not partake of this meal
until all proper thanks are said."

He began the prayer, saying
what he was grateful for—
the good harvest, good health
and allowing him to farm one year more.

Mother was happy, she said,
that the family could gather together.
She prayed that spirit of the day
would continue on forever.

Sister was glad about the blue ribbon
she earned at the county fair.
She said: "Thank you, too, most of all
for parents that really care."

And brother said he was thankful
that he passed his semester test;
and for friends who lent a helping hand
when things weren't going the best.

But the littlest one, barely five,
summed it up best of all:
"I never won a thing. I have no money.
I can't do much 'cause I'm small.

"But one thing for sure I'm thankful for.
Something that you can't even see.
I feel it all the time,
This family's love you spread to me."

To give thanks can be very special.
Still, it carries more meaning yet,
if one counts among the many blessings
those "little things" we tend to forget.

CHAPTER 8

Brrrr, winter's here

Just how cold was it?

On the farm, it was so cold that the usual temptation to knock off that last three-foot icicle hanging from the milk house roof was passed over in favor of a quick retreat to the house for warmth.

It was so cold that the breath of the cows formed a foggy vapor that seemed to freeze in mid-air.

It was so cold that somehow, wearing double everything—socks, gloves, stocking hats—and putting on the warmest of coveralls over the long underwear and blue jeans kept in the warmth for only fifteen minutes or so.

It was so cold on that solemn winter morning that each step you took on the snow-covered ground made a crunching, squeaky sound that sent chills up the back and echoed throughout the entire farmyard.

It was so cold, nobody wanted to get out of bed in the morning as they awakened underneath the warmth of the piles of blankets and quilts. Also, no brave souls wanted to have their feet touch the chilly wood or linoleum-covered floor.

Yes, it got down-to-the-earth, bone-chilling cold in our section of the country. Subzero cold, bitterly cold, with wind chills that were dangerous. Yet on a farm, life doesn't stop for frigid cold or a dastardly blizzard. No way. Livestock must be fed. Cows must be milked. Eggs need to be gathered. Corn must be shelled. Feed must be ground.

Back before there were snowmobile suits, chore time in subzero degrees was always something to dread. Covering our backs were heavily lined jackets, and handy-man yellow cotton gloves only kept our hands warm from the house to the barn. I found that clenching my fists inside the gloves helped keep my hands warmer.

As beings not made of metal and gears but of warm flesh and blood, we had no choice but to go to work out on a cold morning, ready to battle the elements. But the tractors we needed to complete our chores, or the vehicles needed for transportation to neighbors' homes or town, certainly had trouble surviving. I remember many times barely being able to start our Farmall M tractor, sometimes lucky enough to turn over the engine even if it was sheltered from wind chills inside a shed or corn crib. We used that same tractor to pull, by long log chain, the Farmall H (the one with the front end loader) round and round the farm's circle driveway in hopes of getting it started as well.

Matter of fact, we wore a path round and round the farmyard pulling the vehicles on the farm, particularly our old green truck, which we used to move ground feed from one shed to another on the farm. Sooner or later, that truck did start, but not without stopping, tapping frozen gas lines, and being pulled another five rounds to get it restarted.

Because of the cold, the manual transmissions on the automobiles were stiff and had to be worked ferociously at times. I recall many times when my dad had to take off his gloves in the cold and loosen nuts or bolts to work on the engines, only to have gasoline spill out on his skinned knuckles, which made the frigid conditions seem even worse.

The heat houser on the Farmall M did the trick for the most part, keeping the bitter wind chill from frosting the upper extremities of our bodies. With its canvas on the right and left sides of the tractor seat, and the plastic that acted as a windshield in front of the steering wheel, you were hemmed in quite well, but there wasn't a lot of room for movement.

The biggest worries, according to my dad, were making sure that the water hydrants were in working order and that the livestock could still drink without having to battle the ice buildup on top of their water tanks. Inside the cow tank, we had an old cast iron coal-heating unit that when operating would melt the thick ice. It was fueled by clumps of black coal we had delivered to the farm. First, the coal had been broken down to fit snugly into the back compartment of the heater. A hammer usually worked well in breaking up the coal.

Kerosene was sprinkled over the coal and a match was thrown into the heating compartment. As the fire burned, the black smoke billowed out of the stove pipe attached to the cast iron heater, rising above the barn. It had a distinct gassy odor and it caught the attention of the cattle. Eventually, the three-inch ice around the water heater gave way, and then the thaw spread throughout the whole tank.

What was fun, I thought, was taking the chunks of ice that had broken free and smashing them on the concrete apron near the water tank.

One difficult task in the middle of a cold winter was climbing inside the silo chute, crawling through the small opening into the silo, grabbing a pitch fork or a pick axe, and throwing the silage through the door and down the chute where it landed with a thud in chunks on the feed room floor. The axe was needed to break through the frozen top layer of frosted silage. Sometimes the chunks were so big, each toss through the door made a thundering noise as the silage took a free fall down the covered chute. The silage ice chunks had to again be broken down so that the cattle could eat it, flavored on top with a layer of crushed corn. The cold in the silo made the echoes sound extremely loud.

Other than the farmhouse, the warmest place in the winter had to be the barn filled with the cows and calves that provided enough body heat so that we could do our milking chores without our heavy coats and gloves. The barn door was heavily frosted on the inside. You could take a finger and scrape your name on that big sliding door. When the door opened on a brisk cold night or frigid morning, a wave of hot air met the cold, and warm vapor greeted you right in the face. The cats cuddled near their milk dish. It was just so toasty warm there.

It wasn't so warm in the hayloft on a cold winter's night. There were open windows up there, which didn't stop the snow and cold from entering. Climbing the ladder to the loft and lifting open the hayloft door above, it wasn't uncommon to have some snow fall through and land on the back of the neck. Once up there, you'd have to shake some of the ice and frost off the bales of hay and throw it down the chutes, the open windows sometimes being guarded by an owl that would scare the heck out of you. It was probably looking for mice inside the hayloft.

The cow yard had its share of frozen animal waste that made it quite difficult to maneuver the milk cart to and from the milk house. You had to make sure that the cart didn't upend, spilling the night or morning's milk profits. How those milk cans would clang together! It was our morning alarm clock—my dad's way of telling us that it was time to get to work and commence the milking chores.

On a cold winter night, the light from the moon glowed on the snow and gave the farm fields such a picturesque appearance. Drifts from blizzards piled as high as ten feet in the field driveways at times. The day after a blizzard, the Farmall H and its front end loader were put to work making paths so that the farm equipment and feed truck could be moved from one place to another without getting stuck. Chains would be attached to the rear tractor wheels and rattle as the tractor made its passes.

The snow would be pushed into high piles, which made great sledding for the children. Paths the width of the car would be chiseled in the driveway so that the parents could reach the gravel road that passed our house. And a path would be made from the garage straight to the house, so that family members didn't need to walk through the snow to get to the car—the car would be brought right up to the house.

Rides into town could not be taken for granted. We had to wait for the snowplows to clear a path to the main blacktop road that would take us the four miles into town. School days were a waiting game most of the time. Sometimes blizzards would crop up so fast during the day, while we were in school, that early out wasn't soon enough.

We always made it back home, but at times it took someone sticking their head out the window to alert the driver about being too close to the ditches. And on days when we knew a snowstorm was approaching, we'd stock up with food essentials from the town's local grocery stores, or attempt an extra trip into town to the local elevator for some

Snow drifts reached great heights during blizzards on the northeast Iowa farm, but nothing that a good reliable tractor, endloader, and determined driver couldn't handle. Rudy Hackenmiller moves snow to make the driveway passable.

extra feed, just in case we couldn't dig out for a few days or more.

Cold mornings always made the bacon and eggs smell so delicious. That, mixed with the aroma of fresh coffee percolating in a pot on top of the stove, was something you just couldn't forget.

Everyone had his or her own form of heating the house in those days. Some had oil, some had wood. I can remember visiting the neighbors who had, right smack in their living room, what looked like a pot-bellied furnace—throwing out heat where they and my parents would converse about a variety of topics. Oh, how that cast iron stove could throw out the heat, and with a pan of water atop it, bring some humidity into the air.

There were days we'd come in from the cold with frozen digits that stung when hit with warm water. It was a wonder that more of our extremities didn't end up with frostbite. Not that we were careless, or didn't wear as much winter wrap as we should. Our parents were careful with us.

And the animals did just fine. Those outdoors huddled together for warmth. And our brooder house—converted into a farrowing house— was busy, brightened by the heat lamps that gave warmth to the sows delivering their litters. We'd wait for hours during the whole birthing process, keeping the runts close to their mother or keeping the sow from laying on top of the piglets.

It was just so darn cold.

Excuse me for fibbing but...

So cold that the cow's milk turned immediately to ice cream once it left the udder.

So cold that the outdoor DeKalb Seed thermometer ran out of numbers below the zero.

So cold that every word that you spoke outside shattered into a million pieces.

So cold that "when hell freezes over" didn't seem so bad.

So cold that you could tell it was going to be a "five-blanket" night.

So cold that the refrigerator broke down, but the food stayed fine for the rest of the winter.

That's how cold it was. Brrrr. It gives me shivers just thinking about it.

CHAPTER 9

Serving with a smile

The voice penetrated the early morning peaceful slumber. If there ever was a rude awakening, this was it.

"Time to get up. Get up now. Hurry, or you'll be late," Mom called from below the stairs. Everyone else in the family was sleeping comfortably, cozy under their blankets. Not me.

From underneath my pillow, I squinted at the dim-lit alarm clock. It was only 5 a.m. What could be so important to be out of bed by 5 a.m.?

Serving Mass, the 6 a.m. Mass at the Catholic church, that's what. It was my one-week turn in the scheduled altar boy rotation. There was no getting around it.

I grabbed some presentable clothes and headed down the stairs. Mom was ready and waiting, buttering toast and coating it with cinnamon and sugar for me to eat on the run. "Hurry, the car is warmed up. Comb your hair. Make sure your fly is up," she said.

Gosh darn! Most of my friends were still off in slumberland. Why not me? Who volunteered me for this anyway? The town kids only had to walk a short distance to church. I lived eight miles away. Wouldn't it be better if the town kids served all those early Masses?

Mom took no pity on my whining. I growled as we pulled away from the farm driveway and headed into town. The country road we took to town was deserted. Nothing on the way to look at except smoke billowing out country household chimneys on this brisk winter morning.

Maybe we'd see a dead possum or raccoon on the side of the road, run over by a car earlier in the night. It WAS still night, you know.

We got to the church with about ten minutes to spare. There, the regulars of the congregation were already in the pews reciting aloud prayers. I swore I was going to ask the minister, "Does God have a wake-up call for this early in the morning? Will He really be listening?" But I chickened out.

I put on a long black cassock pulled from hangers inside a rectory closet. Over it went the bright white surplus. Then my partner and I lit the altar candles. Minutes later, the parish pastor arrived full of pep and vigor, eager to start the Mass. Such a morning person he was.

I wanted to be an altar boy since second grade, envious of the older boys who appeared so well mannered and respected. It was a privilege to serve Mass: to ring the bells near the altar, to march in processions, to light the tall candles without burning down the church, and to carry the burning incense.

But it wasn't like you could walk up to the parish priest and demand to be allowed to serve Mass. There was intense training involved.

I remember sitting on the school steps with older Mass servers, who had the task of teaching newcomers to memorize many Latin sentences. There were responses that had more than one or two sentences. For me, it might has well have been a litany. There was protocol to follow, procedures and other responsibilities to learn. It was a serious obligation, this altar boy stuff.

The goal? To eventually serve Mass on Holy Saturday, Sundays, Christmas, Palm Sunday, Easter, May Crowning—duties held by the more experienced altar boys. Elementary servers marched in processions. In the back of their minds, mothers secretly envisioned their altar boy going even further than beyond their pews, possibly being called to the priesthood.

Another privilege of being an older altar boy was that the oldest got first choice of the cassock, which was a big deal back then. A cassock was a long, black garment that flowed from the shoulders to the tops of the shoes. It came with buttons, snaps, or Velcro up and down the front.

Most of the time, younger altar boys got stuck with the itchy wool cassocks with the missing buttons or snaps. In that instance, safety pins were used to hold cassocks together in the front. If you were lucky, the cassocks fit perfectly. Most of the time, though, the collar would be tight enough to cut off air circulation and make your face turn a thousand shades of red.

Then again, many times the safety pins opened up and stuck the helpless altar boys during Mass. You just had to absorb those sharp pin jabs, calling it a sacrifice made to God.

Mass servers couldn't have allergies to incense. Sometimes, it got too smoky and the eyes commenced watering, and that's when you decided then or there to remain being an altar boy. I liked the smell of incense, so it never bothered me.

But those early mornings, getting up at 5 a.m. to serve a whole week's shift of morning Masses. Now, that was a different story.

CHAPTER 10

Free time

Naturally, chores and the harvest took a lot of time on the farm. But it wasn't all work and no play. There were plenty of opportunities for fun.

When the cousins came to visit, we'd search the junk pile for tin cans and we'd get out the BB-gun to knock the targets off wooden fence posts. We'd climb the rafters of the corn crib, throw ear corn at pigeons, or pretend we were having a rodeo and we'd ride on the backs of the larger calves.

The aunts and uncles would be inside the house, playing a card game or just talking over a cup of coffee and a piece of cake or homemade pie.

Our yard was big enough to schedule some softball games among cousins or neighbors. Sometimes it was the girls against the guys. Truth be told, the boys had a tough time holding their own in these games because country girls could play just as hard and hit and field as well.

Sometimes Dad and the uncles would come out and join the game. But, as would normally happen, while the children played, the aunts and uncles worked with my parents in other activities—butchering the roosters or collecting the sweet corn planted next to the field corn on the east forty acres.

When the evening milking chores were finished on a Sunday night in the summer, the siblings would walk or ride our bicycles to the neighbors for softball games. We'd play until nobody could see the ball anymore, usually home by 9:30 and back in time to catch some of the fireflies flittering in the night sky.

If we were lucky enough, we were allowed to participate in the nearby town's summer recreation program—playing various stages of organized Little League games. Back then it was the Wee Wees, on to the Pee Wees, and then Midgets. A neighbor and I pedaled our bicycles enthusiastically about six miles to town for the practices and the games, but our tired legs would be churning again with less enthusiasm on the trip back home.

The trick was to cruise fast past the homes along the route that had aggressive, nipping farm dogs. Sometimes we'd carry a stick, or use our bats, to fend off the attacks on our heels.

I loved baseball. One of my most memorable birthday presents was a baseball and a glove. It was given at a birthday party among neighbors, and during a pick-up game we used the new baseball. Somebody whacked the ball into a nearby ditch riddled with weeds and ruts. I didn't find that rubber-coated baseball that day, even after saying a prayer to St. Anthony (patron saint of lost causes) about a hundred times. About six years later while mowing the ditch, the ball was found—worse for the wear, but still quite a treasure, and I rejoiced in having it back again.

Sometimes we had to make our own fun. The girls, I recall, would always put their imaginations to work and outline a house with rooms, framing the walls of their house with piles of freshly mowed grass. There were times we'd rake the grass and pile it high, just as we did the leaves in the fall, and leap into the heap.

In the winter, with new snow on the ground, there was time for sledding runs on the driveway, or playing "Fox and Goose" as we made footprints and paths in the snow. Also in the winter, we'd hike out to the diverted acres farm pond and put on the ice skates, gliding until our faces and hands were numb from the cold.

Many farms had tire swings that hung from the strong branches of a tree. Ours hung on an old evergreen limb. As soon as you sat in the swing, you couldn't avoid getting a whiff of the pine and sappy smell of the tree.

It was just as fun watching Dad make the swing, as he turned the tire inside out and cut the holes needed for person to grip while swinging. With the rider in the tire swing, we'd push on both ends and get the tire swing reaching as high as the lower branches of the tree. Sometimes those who had a tolerance for going around in circles would sit in the tire and spin, winding the rope round and round. Eventually, the tire swing rope could twist no more. The rider would lift his feet and let the tire swing twirl him around until he was so dizzy he could hardly walk straight.

In earlier years, fathers made toys for their children. One I can remember was a custom-made wooden rod that pushed a small steel circular rim around the driveway, the object being to see who could go the greatest distance without the rim falling to the ground. Some fathers made stilts, too, for their children and issued a challenge for them to walk without falling.

Some Sunday afternoons, we'd get the garden fork and dig for worms near the granary or garden, the slippery crawlers to be used as bait. We'd head out to a nearby river or stream to fish for some bluegills, crappies, bullheads, or catfish. Dad would park his truck in a field driveway along the roadway out of harm's way, and we'd have to hike about a half-mile or so to the river. We'd have fried pan fish that night for dinner if we caught enough.

On our farm and many others, it wasn't uncommon to see a basketball hoop attached to the garage or to the doors of the crib or barn. Some even had basketball courts in their hayloft. Whenever there was a spare second or two, we'd get out our basketballs and play a game of "horse" or just shoot around. The basketball hoops might not have been regulation height, but it was fun being able to dunk the basketball or hit the fade-aways on a slightly lower hoop. Some days the make-do basketball court would be muddy or greasy. Then we'd wait until later in the day or early in the morning, when the ground froze, to hone our shooting skills. If we didn't, then the walls of the corn crib would be marked up with the imprint of the basketball in hundreds of places, which was irritating to Dad, I'm sure.

Some Sunday afternoons we'd take turns hosting sandlot tackle football games with classmates and neighbors. We were fortunate to have a narrow playing field strip near Mom's garden. Other neighboring places we played on also had gravel to contend with—which smarted quite a bit when one was tackled on the gritty substance.

Today, you don't hear a lot about neighbors getting together to talk, playing card games. Sandlot games appear to be uncommon. Neighbors don't often share their leisure minutes. Many don't even know who their neighbors are.

After the milking chores were done, on a Friday or Saturday night, parents would go to a dance hall to polish their waltzing and polka dancing skills. As the children grew older, they too found the dance floor a good place to socialize and meet new people and new friends.

Parents would also socialize through organized card parties—sometimes held on New Year's Eve or the holidays. While the parents played their card games, the children would play board games or watch the bowl football games on television.

A form of entertainment in the early 1960s was the black and white television, capturing the interest of this young group.

Television, in its early black-and-white stages, offered some respite from a listless evening. Color television had not yet gained national appeal. Sometimes it was just nice for the folks to sit in an easy chair and read magazines such as Wallaces Farmer or Farm Journal to pass the time away or keep up with the latest in farm technology. Family members would race to the mailbox to see what came their way—the weekly newspaper, letters from relatives and friends, school magazines, and more.

The best times on the farm were watching someone hit a softball over somebody's cow yard fence (usually an automatic home run), or throwing a big rubber ball over the roof of the house or garage and having somebody on the other side try to catch it. It was a real gas to have somebody break through the arms during a game of Red Rover or to have a corncob fight in the corn crib.

There were no video games back then. You had to make your own fun. And most were able to do that just fine.

CHAPTER 11

Women at work

Keep in mind that women, too, fulfilled important roles on the family farm. Some worked just as hard, or harder, at completing the chores ahead of them. They could drive tractors just as well as the men, work side by side with the butchering and raising of the livestock, clean out the gutters or stalls, milk the cows, harvest the crop, and other tasks.

In some instances, large families had enough boys to toil in the fields and livestock buildings. But in some known families there were no sons and plenty of daughters, so the girls had to help manage the farm chores.

Not only did the mother of the farm family have to deal with the baking, the laundry, the transportation, and the rearing of the children, she was often called upon to watch over the flock of chickens and gather and clean the eggs, to drive the tractor at baling time, or bring home loads of corn or oats from the fields. Mothers were in charge of the family garden, the rows of sweet corn, the butchering of the roosters and separating the cream.

Just as soon as Mother was done cleaning her house, she would be putting straw into the hen house nests or watering down the hogs on a hot and humid day. About the time she collected the last tomato off the vine from the spacious garden or picked the last apple off the ground, she'd be ready to wash the Surge milking buckets and sanitize all the equipment so that the milk quality from the cows would pass inspection.

When her husband fell ill and had to refrain from working outdoors, she'd chip in or take the lead, with or without the children, in getting the farm chores done so that life on the farm wouldn't miss a beat.

When she was finished hanging the sheets and diapers on the clothesline, she'd be helping her husband chase stray cattle into their proper places. When night fell, she'd give the toddlers their baths and tuck them into bed, and then head out into the brooder houses and keep the birthing sows from rolling over on any of the sow's litter, often singling out the runt and bringing it back to good health.

When she had to get up early to make breakfast for her own children and send them off to school, or take them by car to school herself, she'd also make sure that there was enough of a start in preparing food in the house to feed the neighbors who were coming to the farm to help fill the silo, to help combine the oats, or to help bale the hay or straw.

Once a sick child had to be taken to town to visit a doctor for a shot or medicine, she'd return to the farm and make sure she supplied plenty of care and doting on the child, then make sure not to neglect the child's favorite kitten or dog so that they, too, would miss any affection.

I wouldn't be surprised if other women's schedules were similar to our mother's. The men and boys would head out in the morning to milk the cows, and when the chores were done, there would be a heap of fried bacon and eggs waiting on a hot platter for all to consume. The coffee pot would be percolating and if we were lucky enough, there would be frosted cinnamon rolls as we all gathered around the table for breakfast. Before coming into the house we brought in a gallon or two of milk from the big cream cans inside the cooler. Mom or one of the daughters would skim the cream off the top of the containers and use the cream for baking or for the parents' cup of coffee.

After breakfast, the boys went back outside to help with the chores and get started on other projects of the day—grinding feed, cleaning out livestock buildings, putting rings in the screaming hogs' snouts, harvesting, or whatever else was planned.

The female siblings in the house would begin their tasks for the day—cleaning the milking equipment brought over from the barn, gathering the eggs from the hen house, washing the eggs so that they'd be ready for the town's egg buyer when he came for pick up. Mother would begin the process of baking bread, making dozens of loaves at a time. One day during the week was designated as bread-making day, and it wasn't uncommon for her to bake twenty or more loaves during the day in addition to coffee cakes, caramel rolls, and other tasty treats.

Wash days usually fell on Tuesdays and Thursdays. Some farms had two washing machines. One of the tubs would be used to wash all the manure-laden clothing stacked in piles in the basement of the house. Another would be used for all the delicates, the towels, the dress clothes for church or school, and more. Included in the laundry chores were the patching of the coveralls, the repair of the loose buttons, stitching a tear in the pockets, and much more. Having a reliable sewing machine on the farm was a necessity.

The gardening chores, such as the weeding and the pea-picking, the sweet corn husking, and the tomato gathering, usually fell to the women. However, whenever some of the sons had nothing to do and were idly standing around, there were always potatoes to dig, rows to till or hoe, bags to carry, or apples to pluck from the heights of tall trees. Everyone pitched in, in other words. There were really no gender divisions. Everyone had their own tasks.

Farming wasn't always such a profit-making venture. Women often had to help keep the operation afloat with paying jobs of their own. For instance, my mother served as a waitress at a restaurant in a neighboring town. Some worked as secretaries or clerks in the home town's businesses. Some were school teachers. While mother worked elsewhere, daughters took on more roles—the making of the bread and preparation of the meals, the house cleaning, the lawn mowing, and much more in addition to babysitting the younger siblings. They'd bring out a plate of cookies and a cool, refreshing drink to the field workers.

Mothers also seemed to be the ones arranging all the social entertainment on the farms. There were new recipes to try out, new desserts to tempt the taste buds. She'd be the one inviting company to the farm, the one who would consent to hosting the 4-H meetings or sweet corn husking harvests among the aunts, uncles, and cousins. She'd be in charge of the guest list for the card parties. She'd fret over the church circle meetings.

When it was time for making the sausages or butchering the roosters, she'd enlist the help of her own brothers and sisters or neighbors, and make sure that her guests would take home plenty of the produce.

Mothers would make darn sure of that.

CHAPTER 12

Trips to town

The town, although only a short distance from the thousands of acres of farmland surrounding it, was a place that was so crucial to the farm's survival and also to the spirits of the people on the homestead.

Farmers and townsmen normally co-existed in a cordial way. They had to. Both depended greatly on each other. We, as children, always knew when it was time for parents to head to the nearby town when it wasn't a Sunday.

On Sundays, it was automatic, as we loaded the family into the cleanest mechanically able vehicle and filled our pew at the church services. And the children went to the parish school in all but the summer months.

But that was just church and school for us. Going other spots in the town was an even greater thrill. So when Dad would shave during the middle of the week, and Mother had her best clothes laid out and ready to wear for the next day, you knew that a trip to town, or to another place, was coming.

The town we frequented had a population of about 600, an even greater number before my time.

For farm business trips, dads would take the children to the local elevator, where the ten or more employees always knew the person walking into the building by his first name. It smelled of ground feed, and there was grain dust on the floor of the main office. On the chalk board, above the scale that weighed the wagon load or trucks bringing in or taking out the grain, were the most recent posted grain prices. But as a child, my eyeballs were glued to the round glass ball on the top of the counter. It was filled with peanuts. One penny in the slot, a short turn, and the palms of the hand would be filled with the salty treats.

Against the wall, I recall, was a soda machine that carried flavors such as root beer, orange, or strawberry. No diet drinks. If a dad wanted to treat his child, he'd stick a dime into the machine, lift up the lid, drag the selected beverage to a certain spot, and then lift the bottle straight out. He'd then find the cap remover on the side of the machine and he'd join his son in a treat of sugary thirst-quenching—most refreshing on a hot day. We'd sit, and I enjoyed listening to the conversation that ranged from crop prices to church meetings and more. Afterward, we'd get our fill of feed from the elevator and bring it home, where it would last for days in the box of the truck until the next trip into town.

Near the town elevator were livestock holding pens, where livestock producers would bring their fatted pigs or cattle and arrange to have them shipped to destinations for whatever dollars the market would bring to us. Normally, we'd hire a livestock hauler to take the animals to the livestock holding pens in town, and we'd follow the hauler into town. There, the owner of the livestock business and Dad would negotiate their fees, chat and laugh, and then get on with business as another truck load of livestock came into the holding pen area. People sure talked a lot back then.

Nearby, we'd make a stop at the local creamery. The big-boxed creamery trucks, filled with milk cans, would pull up to a platform outside the creamery. The milkman, or milk collector, would open the door to the truck box and place each filled can on a conveyor that would move along from outside to inside the building where the milk would be dumped and cans cleaned and returned by conveyor back to the truck. While there, the creamery manager and Dad would talk about the milk prices and milk checks would be doled out. Dad would remember that he had better come home with butter, or else he'd have nothing on his toast for the next morning's breakfast.

Now, most farmers had practice doing their own equipment repair. But there were some things that just couldn't be fixed by a farmer's own hands. It had to be either repaired by an experienced welder or tinker, or replaced by parts available from the town's implement dealer. And if it was such a great, profitable year and there was enough in the account to buy some new machinery, then there would be gleaming combines, new tractors, new disks or drags, plows, and other used implements on the lot cleaned up and shining, just ripe for the picking.

It was amazing, when walking to the counter of the implement dealer, how they knew exactly what part they had in stock and what was available. Walk inside and it smelled like brand new tires. Most of the time, the business owners would call you into their office and talk business. They had a healthy supply of calendars, key chains, pens, and pencils that they would hand out to whoever needed them. In the bigger shed of the implement dealer's business was the repair shop, where skilled mechanics would piece together items such as blown tractor engines.

There would sometimes be stops at the veterinarian's office to pick up medicine for the cowherd for the treatment of mastitis or treating the hogs for scours and other diseases. You could smell the medicine—it seemed to have the same scent as the doctor's office next door.

Home remedies for parents and children on the farm didn't always do the trick. The smell of the medicine in a doctor's office, and just thinking about that long needle you were likely going to be stuck with, was enough to discourage visits. The doctors and nurses, however, were very friendly and helpful. They were constantly busy doing all phases of medical care, from curing sore throats and tonsils to setting broken arms and casting.

As much as many didn't want to make visits to the doctor an everyday occurrence, going to the dentist office, which was just above the doctor's office, wasn't on anyone's thrill list either, although it was an extreme necessity.

It was a rarity for some fathers to take their families to the cafes or lounges in the town. That seemed reserved for the business workers in the community. But that didn't stop farmers from making visits to the businesses and stocking up on a case of beer or two to bring back home— a welcome taste to adults after a hard day's work. An occasional card game would start up in the taverns and draw some together for a short afternoon of fun.

When plumbing would go wrong in the house, or appliances would malfunction, a trip had to be made to the hardware store for replacement parts or for new items. It was also the place to pick up the propane gas that operated the gas-burning furnace or stove. Broken bolts or the lack of a washer also were on the shopping list.

Trips to the town grocery store were also frequent, but primarily for purchases of cereal, flour, sugar, and other items. Most of the food such as meat, vegetables, bread, and other staples were available on the farm. But I can recall, after eating slice after slice of homemade bread, how nice it would be to taste bread prepackaged from the factories. Once in a while the parents would come home from town with treats from the store, chewy wrapped candy or taffy, as an incentive or treat for the children.

Our community also had the banks, gas stations and bulk fuel delivery, funeral homes, newspaper office, library and city hall, barbershops, fabric and clothing stores, beauty salons, fire department, city jail, and much more. Some other smaller towns had furniture stores, liquor stores, movie theaters, dance halls, and fire department, too. The larger cities were no more than forty-five miles away.

In retrospect, the townspeople and the farmers were friends to the end. There may have been some ill feelings now and then, but it didn't last too long. After all, it was the farmers who provided the eggs and the dairy products to the restaurants and the grain for the purchased feed. It was the savings and loan bank that provided the capital for farmers to continue working the land, and the income farmers made from their sale of products was spent in the nearby community, helping keep businesses alive.

One entity would find it hard to exist without the other. I suppose some townspeople didn't know how to drive a tractor or plow a straight furrow. Then again, farmers might be hard-pressed to know about rising inventories, fixing the television, or making the right decisions on what works best for their line of equipment.

It's like having a machine that has hundreds of different parts, but it must be well-maintained and oiled and treated with respect so that it all works in unison.

That's pretty much how it was back then, and it still holds true today.

CHAPTER 13

The holidays

Sure, each day on the farm the cows needed to be milked, hogs needed to be fed, eggs needed to be collected, and barns needed to be cleaned. The world didn't stand still for holidays or special events.

Memorial Day and Labor Day were working holidays, with positively no Mondays off. Cows never took the day off. Nor did the weeds ever stop growing in the cornfield, nor did the hay stop drying in the hayfield.

But nonetheless, bits and pieces of the holidays were precious. The special part of Memorial Day was going to the church and veterans' services, listening to the gun salutes, and then heading home to a bigger lunch than usual.

Easter, in all its glory, was celebrated with all the decorations and traditions within the Catholic family. Aside from the traditional holiest of church services in which all altar servers and parish members were heavily involved, children also would partake in various other activities at their homes.

Egg coloring, using vinegar and food coloring, involved some patience and plenty of imagination. The good thing about that was that you didn't have to buy the eggs because most of them came from the hen house. There was always a big basket of candy next to the colored eggs on Easter morning.

On Good Friday, the menu usually included all the pancakes you could eat, since meat couldn't be served. Saturday usually was preparation day for late evening church services full of ceremony and candles and burning incense. It was also the time for getting together the food and details for the Easter Sunday meal, which would usually include the inviting of guests that included numerous aunts and uncles, grandparents, and anyone else who could come.

After a fill of Easter eggs and homemade rolls on Sunday morning and Easter Sunday services that followed, we'd come home to a kitchen that smelled of roast beef and ham, potatoes and gravy, and plenty of desserts to choose from. After the meal, we'd chat around the table with guests and get in a family card game that would last until the late afternoon hours or until it was time for the milking chores.

The Fourth of July usually fell on the days when the hay was cut and drying in the field or baling was in process. If there was a break in that action, we could get away for a Fourth of July parade in a nearby town. After the evening milking, the family would pile into the station wagon and make the trip to that same town, where we would climb on our cousin's house roof and get a good view of the fireworks display. Or, the fireworks would be brought to our house. Dad concocted a fireworks shooter—an extra eaves spout. A hole was cut where the string fuse to the firework was lighted. We'd shoot the fireworks through the downspout and over the cornfield where it would light up the sky with brilliant colors. Later in the evening we'd light up the backyard with colorful sparklers.

The corn harvest was usually completed by Thanksgiving, so the traditional holiday meal usually occurred after the milking chores and the last ear corn load of the day went into the corn crib or onto temporary piles. It made the day go a lot better knowing that once we got into that house, there was a scrumptious, wonderful Thanksgiving meal with all the trimmings waiting for us. You never forget that smell. And it's even harder to forget about the taste of turkey, cranberries, casseroles, and pumpkin pie with whipped topping made from scratch.

Company would also sometimes be there—usually an aunt or uncle who had no children of their own who wanted to be with family. They also brought candy treats for their nieces and nephews. All slept very well that Thanksgiving night, but it made it that much harder to get up that next Friday morning for the early milking chores.

One good thing after Thanksgiving was Christmas wasn't that far away. There were numerous events leading up to Christmas—the school Christmas programs, as well as the visits to town to visit Santa Claus as he handed out the hard, colorful ribbon candy, chocolate drops, and for health purposes, an apple. Christmas also brought out the curiosity in many a child, who was always wondering where the parents hid the gifts. Maybe that's why Dad always found more chores than usual for us to do during December, and Mom kept the girls in the kitchen doing more of the cleaning, folding clothes, and making Christmas cutout cookies. The less time we had to think about Christmas gifts, the more their hiding places would be safer.

As a child I found the hiding spot one year—high up in the garage. I found the football that I would be getting and other things that the other siblings would receive. Fact is, when Christmas morning came, it just wasn't the same excitement as before. The suspense was gone. I never went Christmas gift hunting as a child again.

Sometimes Santa would come Christmas Eve, after our supper before we'd go out and do the milking. Everybody would be in the house, and there would be a rap on the window that made us jump about two feet into the air. "Check outside," the parents would say. Outdoors in front of the house were a pile of gifts left by Santa—or maybe a helping neighbor. Many times, though, Santa visits would come on Christmas morning as siblings stood by the upstairs rails at five o'clock in the morning waiting for the word from parents to come down and "get it over with so Dad could get the milking chores finished."

At church, there was a Nativity display that featured a rural setting. Sometimes as Mass servers we had to help with midnight services. In northern Iowa, there was usually snow on the ground, and sometimes it would snow Christmas Eve, adding to the nostalgia.

One of our best Christmas trees at home, I believe, was when the top of an evergreen tree standing tall within the yard was cut to fit inside our living room. It probably was because there wasn't a whole lot of money back then to go out and buy a tree. But it smelled so great and sisters did a good job of decorating it with tinsel and old ornaments. We had many evergreens on the farm, so I'm surprised we didn't lop off more of the fir trees.

Halloween and New Year's celebrations were usually celebrated with neighbors and friends. On the farm, it wasn't very practical going door to door for trick or treat. So parents got together with friends and their families and had their own parties. They talked and played cards while the children bobbed for apples and played other games, also enjoying Halloween treats.

We'd bring in the New Year usually at another neighbor's home, watching the football bowl games into the late evening hours and enjoying snacks. Some of the younger children made it to midnight; others didn't, and their slumbering bodies had to be carried to their cars and into their beds once they returned home.

Outside of the regular holidays, many families considered numerous events as days off from the tedious work on the farm. Family reunions generally took up much of a Sunday meal and afternoon fun.

There were First Communion and Confirmation celebrations. Graduations and their receptions were always special, too. The May high school graduations were particularly memorable because of the surroundings on the farm—the lilac trees were in full bloom and the peonies were opening up to full color. Ham sandwiches were plentiful, with the buns made from scratch with loving hands by Mother. The grass was mowed the day before, so all was fresh in the yard and garage.

Yes indeed. Holidays on the farm, then, were shared by family, relatives, and friends, which made the celebrations fun. The more, the merrier, they said.

I can still see my parents toasting to the New Year, or the siblings ripping gift wrapping off of presents stacked underneath the Christmas tree. It's what wonderful memories are made of.

CHAPTER 14

Climbing to the top

Silo-filling time on the farm was a thrill for those who were keenly interested in tractor models and horsepower. That's because, just as it was a neighborly project in those earlier years to help each other with the threshing of oats, in later years neighbors would help with the silo-filling venture.

And they would bring with them all the tractors and silage wagons (from rear unloading to more modern front auger unloading) they had on their farms. There was so much variety of tractors, small to large, and old or modern farm implements to view.

When it came to our turn, a farmer and his family down the road, a true Oliver tractor fan, provided the corn chopper, while another neighboring farmer provided the blower and the pipes to shoot the silage into the silos. It was a verbal or handshake agreement that the farmers along the road would help each other out to make the silage harvest run smooth and quickly—usually taking place in the middle of fall when the school year had just commenced and the little children were "out of harm's way."

There were many types of shared arrangements between landowners back then. Farmers sometimes relied on others to be partners in the purchase of new or used implements. For some, it might have been a joint purchase of a baler. Others might have agreed to go in together to buy a new or used combine or hay conditioner. Farmers also counted upon neighbors' custom work, often hiring someone to shell their ear corn or open up a cornfield with a mounted two-row corn picker.

Assuredly, each farmer had his or her own tractor allegiance, his or her own pride and joy, a reason to boast about beauty and power. In addition to the Oliver tractors, there were John Deere models, perhaps an Allis Chalmers or Massey Fergusons in the mix, and Farmall tractors— all were used in the silo-filling tasks.

There were more Farmall tractors on our farm at the time of silo filling, since the majority of the neighbors involved had carried that model. The Farmalls came in all sizes—from the Super C and B models to the Farmall H and M tractors and eventually bigger International Harvester models.

Many area farm boys or girls learned to operate a tractor at an early age by driving around feed wagons in wide open fields or moving along slowly driving a baler during the hay harvest. Most started out sitting on the lap of the father, allowed to turn the steering wheel while Dad operated the clutches and gear shift.

It wasn't that difficult. Primarily it was knowing how to shift for speed and pulling, how to work the throttle and drive a straight line without too much effort. Thankfully, power steering made tractor operation a whole lot easier. A higher degree of difficulty in tractor operation occurred when backing a wagon into a tight spot in a shed, when pulling a plow, or when moving at a snail's pace when cultivating corn or soybeans, careful not to wipe out a length or two of rows.

When silo-filling rolled around, usually once the corn ears had developed with a degree of milkiness and the stalks were not so dried out, farmers would leave their own homestead throughout the ensuing days helping their neighbors top off one, two, or even three silos. They would leave after the morning milking and return about the time evening chores commenced, which made for a very long day.

Fortunately for children who enjoyed the harvest, not everything in silo-filling had been done while we were in school. Once we got off the school bus, we knew the neighboring crew had moved operations to our place because the fence gates to the cornfields were wide open and the cattle yard was bare.

We watched from a distance as the silo blower and pipes, moved from another farm to ours, were put into place. The pipes reached high into the sky. Dad would scale the tall silo, lock in the pipes, and position the spout so the silage would pile to the center of the silo.

Later years, that same assignment, and the leveling off of the top, would go to his older boys. Most silos had rungs with handles to grip and ladders that would lead the climber to a platform attached to the silo's top. It was a thrill to view the countryside from atop the silo, scanning the land and seeing farms spread out in all directions as far as the eyes could see. It was as close to the heavens one could physically get.

Stalks of corn are in the shadows of a concrete silo on the Hackenmiller farm.

Once the silo filling commenced, one person would run the chopper in the fields, and the rest of the neighboring farmers would drive their tractor and silage wagons back and forth to the blower. The younger adults helped unload the silage into the blower auger, chipping away at the packed, open back end of the silage wagon with pick forks while an apron in the wagon slowly moved the silage to the rear.

The whole silo-filling process on the farm took at least two full days, and that required serving a hearty meal at noon for the workers. All operations of the silo-filling would cease at the dinner call and each participant would crowd around the house sink to wash up, then gather around the table to enjoy Mom's helpings of chicken or roast beef, potatoes, vegetables from the garden, and more. The meal would be topped off with a fresh piece of pie or cobbler, and mixed in was a healthy helping of good conversation on a variety of topics.

Each man worked off their meal in the afternoon hours as he hopped back on his own tractor. The silo-filling work resumed where it left off. Out in the field, corn stubble replaced the tall stalks, with plenty of corn in adjoining fields still standing awaiting the ear corn harvest and for filling the crib bins later in the fall.

Each night, parents cautioned their children to stay away from the freshly filled silo. Gas emitted from the fresh silage was deadly. Sparrows that hung around the silo were found dead on the ground, as were mice that crawled into the silo's attached feed shed. Obviously, that was all the incentive we needed to stay away.

Once the last wagon was unloaded and the blower and pipes dismantled, things really quieted down on the farm. The neighbors said their goodbye, and filed out of the driveway one by one with their tractors and wagons, turning onto the rural gravel road that connected them to each other—either moving on to another farm up the road or returning their equipment home permanently until the next grand show of tractors—err—silo-filling event the following year.

Wheels A-Turning

Corn acres have turned golden
and combines strip the fields,
knifing through the clean rows.
Hope grows for a great yield.

Into wagons the auger pours
the grain 'til there's no more room.
Tractors pull loads down the road.
The mid-afternoon sun will fade soon.

On to the town elevator, and the scales tip.
This year's bounty is tallied.
It was more than first projected,
the farmer's spirit seems rallied.

While back at the home place
the fields are picked totally clean.
Fall tillage buries this year's roots,
as only remnants of the crops are seen.

So the annual fall ritual is over.
It's one of the busiest times of the year.
Wheels are constantly in motion
when harvesting is in full gear.

The farmer's mind is turning, too.
Despite times not as good as before,
maybe things will pick up in the spring
when they take to the fields once more.

CHAPTER 15

The garden of plenty

I don't know if Mother scanned seed catalogs months and months before planting that first seed in her special garden. Then again, why would she? Most of the large gardens on the country farms didn't have elaborate or foreign plants, but primarily contained the essentials for feeding the families of those serving the land.

That meant plenty of green beans, potatoes, carrots, peas, cabbage, parsnips, strawberries, squash, onions, tomatoes, sweet corn, and perhaps some melons as special treats.

Some of the gardens got as large as half an acre or more. Guess it all depended on the size of the family. If there were only two on the farm, perhaps a small patch behind the henhouse would do. That would never be enough for a large family.

Our garden was tailored to feed a family of twelve. Preparation began well before spring. Over the winter, manure from the cattle yard was spread over the patch of plowed ground—a good supply of nutrients for the soil. Seed potatoes were purchased from a dealer in a nearby farm and put into the cellar, hibernating before the sprouts shot through the eyes of the tasty vegetable.

At the same time the field corn was planted, some farmers made it a point to plant sweet corn on the outside rows, most of the time along the fence lines. Usually, sweet corn was in demand not only for the family, but also for relatives and friends who didn't have the room to grow their own garden. So there always had to be enough planted to feed plenty.

One reason why few went hungry on the family farm was because of the huge garden that grew sweet corn, potatoes, and numerous other vegetables. Visible in the background is the dairy barn in its late stages.

After the corn and the soybeans were planted in the fields and the frost gone permanently, it was time to disk the plowed ground of the garden and then pull the drag over the soil to smooth it over. Once the soil reached the right temperature, or there was a break from the April showers, work commenced on planting the garden.

The potatoes were the first to be planted. It was a tradition to sow the potatoes on Good Friday, as long as it didn't fall too early in the year. To make the rows straight, many concocted their own methods. Our method was to use two metal rods (normally used for electric fencing) and tie baling twine on each, stretching the twine over the length of the garden. We'd follow the tightened twine with our hoe and drop in the potatoes.

The same monotonous procedure was followed for the onions, the beans, the carrots, and the peas. It was a lot of bending, a lot of calculating, and a lot of digging, but it was worth the trouble when the bounty was harvested in the fall.

During the summer, flowers bloomed around the garden. Some gardens were bordered by peonies, others daisies or other wildflowers. These delightful, fragrant beauties served as barriers around the garden and made it look fruitful even on a bad year when early frost or disease got the best of the plants.

Caring for the garden, from the first sprouting seeds to the end of the harvest, was a task shared by the whole family.

Creamed peas for Sunday dinner were a favorite. The Saturday afternoon before, shucking of the peas took place outside—the pods were recycled as feed and fed to the hogs, as was much of the waste from the garden. It's hard to imagine how much more the yield of peas would have been if so many hadn't been eaten while the shucking went on. A good share never made it to the dinner table, but there was always plenty planted for freezing.

Another time-consuming task was the digging of the potatoes in the fall. The potato fork got its workout as parents and children dug into the soil, well below the dying plant, and turned over what would be a multitude of spuds. The potatoes would be gathered and thrown into a bin, where they would later be sacked or stored in the cellar and saved for a Sunday meal.

Sweet corn harvest usually turned out to be a family affair, as aunts and uncles would join in on the picking, the peeling off of the husks, and the canning that was going on in the kitchens. Normally, it was a big social event—with all the talking, all the world's problems were solved in one way or another. The children joined in the festivities—some not liking it at all because it wasn't what they considered fun. They'd throw the spoiled ears at each other, or wouldn't make an effort to get all the corn silk out of the ear, leaving it to the parents at the canning site.

But oh, who would be the first at the table to sample the ear of sweet corn, with butter dripping and tempered with just the right amount of salt. The children, of course, couldn't wait for that first bite off the cob. The spoils—the husks, cobs, or other leftovers—would get thrown over the hog yard fence, where the swine would dine.

The garden was hard work. It required constant cultivating—first with hoe and later on with the gas-fed tiller that made the work between the rows a whole lot easier. There was also continuous weeding. That was a chore left to the children, usually as some sort of punishment. When we did something that was rightfully punishable, we weren't sent to our rooms. We were sent to the garden for weed-pulling duty.

Canning was an essential skill acquired by the mother to feed the family through the winter months. The task involved a lot of jars, a lot of boiling kettles, and a lot of sweat in the kitchen. If it wouldn't spoil in a jar, it was canned.

We'd help ourselves to a tomato or two, picked right off the vine. Often, the tomatoes were canned into juices for drinking or for stewing.

Heavy indulgence, however, came during berry-picking time. Family members would scour the strawberry patch and fill containers to the brim, helping themselves to a mouthful or two. We were lucky there were enough strawberries left for toppings on cakes and pie fillings, by the time the delicious berries were all harvested.

In the ditches, growing wild, were raspberries. Each year a sign was posted with the ditch that lined the gravel road to our farm that asked for "No spraying." Doing so would ruin the berry harvest.

In the spring, the peonies would begin to bloom along the garden. Ants would crawl all over the blossoms and it was a mystery to see the busy insects at work. If you sniffed the blossoms by holding them to your nose, then you'd have to be careful that the ants wouldn't hop on board your body. The smell of fresh lilacs spread a sweet fragrance throughout the farm, drawing bumblebees and butterflies.

In the fall, after the last of the melons, squash, and pumpkins had been harvested and the huckleberries removed, it was time to let the garden die by way of the moldboard plow, so that it could be reborn in the spring.

CHAPTER 16

Sold!

"The following items will be sold at public auction on the farm located from Osage, Iowa, seven miles northwest on Highway 218 and four miles north on gravel; or from Stacyville, Iowa, three miles west on A-23 and half-mile south; or from St. Ansgar, Iowa, four miles east on Highway 218 and four miles north on gravel. Sales starts promptly at 10:01 a.m., with lunch served on the grounds by St. Mary's Southwest Country Circle."

That was written on the auction bill when farm machines and relics of my parents' farm were sold in April of 1987. Listing of the homeowner's addresses were how many of the auction bills started out, eventually posted in banks, grocery stores, and grain elevators, and published in some form throughout area newspapers and shoppers. This auction bill had a nice side note to it from the area auctioneers who worked at sales throughout nearby communities.

"This is a three-generation farm. Most of all the machinery is still here. Rudy updated machinery and it is clean and field ready," the auctioneers wrote on the bill.

The tractor list on the auction bill had four tractors—all Farmalls, from a Super C tractor, on up to a Farmall 400, Farmall 560, and Farmall 760 with a cab, all gas tractors. Then it listed the International plow and International baler, the Gehl grinder mixer (with extra screens), and the New Idea manure spreader in good condition. There was a Kiefer Built stock trailer in A-1 shape, John Deere planter, International cultivator,

Stan Hoist chisel plow, Lindsay four-section drag, Owatonna windrower, four-bar side rake, Glenco field cultivator, Farmhand front unload feeder wagon, Parker gravity box with Kasten running gear, Dakon gravity box with Knowls running gear, Mayrath auger, Tox-o-Wik corn dryer, Winco portable generator, and a Van Dale silo unloader.

Old plows drew quite a bit of interest at the farm auction, particularly from the Amish that congregated at the site.

Do you see a pattern here? It was a hodge-podge of machinery ranging from a wide spectrum of companies—featuring well-known and not-so-known trademark names. Most implements were obtained by Dad from used farm equipment lots and other farm auctions.

Dad, like other farmers, had attended many auctions in his lifetime. He and others weren't timid about using the older equipment over some of the more modern equipment they also possessed. Old machinery seemed to be a matter of pride for them—the icing on the cake for many. Just like today's car collectors who enjoy riding the Thunderbirds, the Roadrunners, the Camaros, the Model Ts, the coupes, or other vehicles driven long ago.

Everything had a purpose, even if it was made from scratch. If Dad had a task to perform, but no tools or gimmick that he could buy to get the job done, he, like other farmers, had the ingenuity and skills to go ahead and invent one on his own.

Those inventions, too, eventually got auctioned off, with or without patents. That was the way with my father. That's what many farmers did when they couldn't afford the higher-priced implements. They made do with what they had, even resurrecting machinery that hadn't run in decades.

But what I liked most on the auction bill was the miscellaneous items listing. This tale-telling list showed the character of the farmer and his family, detailing a little insight into a family of generations. Listed on my parents' farm auction bill, was a 1932 Chevrolet transmission from an old family car (which was parked on blocks for many years underneath one of the apple trees near the brooder houses).

This old vehicle was a play car to the siblings who enjoyed getting behind the wheel pretending to go for a drive to visit their cousins or other neighbors. They poked and punched the instrument panel, imitating sounds of the dead engine. One sibling had to be treated for numerous stings because she didn't know about the wasp nests that had formed in the back seat of the vehicle. Those wasps were angry and didn't take kindly to visitors.

There were many other items at this auction that gained the interest of the Amish community, who shunned the use of electricity and thrived on the simple, but hard-working way of life. They made their bids on such items as the buggy tongue, horse harnesses, one horse-pulled walking cultivator and a wooden beam walking plow, an iron beam walking plow, old iron seats, old planter stakes, a cowboy tank heater, old steel wheel wagon, iron piles and wagon wheels of all sizes, side splitter meat saw, butcher hooks, milk can cart, hand corn planter, hay knives, hand potato planter, two very good chicken crates, wood burning kitchen cook stove, old cream separator, and stationary buzz saw with an extra blade.

On the list was a small Shriners Honda Bike 150 that was used by my two brothers until it could no longer function and needed extensive repair. It wasn't a Harley, but it was sure fun.

On the auction bill, offering something to chuckle about, was the new Schweiss chicken picker with electric motor and the warm morning heater stove. This stove warmed the siblings who crowded around it on those subzero days. The old Maytag wringer washing machine, used in the basement of the house, was also on the auction bill.

There were more typical farm items listed for sale, seen on almost every farm in the county, such as a portable air compressor, log chains, tractor chains, electric fencer along with electric fence posts and wire and insulators, heat lamps, tools such as a socket set and hand wrenches, grease tubs and oil, bench vise, fuel barrels, barbed and woven wire, feed bunks, hay bunks, small hog troughs and feeders, welder complete with arcs, and a trash burner.

Just thinking about the heat lamps reminded me of the times filling the small water trays and feed troughs in the brooder houses for the baby chicks that stayed warm under the glow of the light. The electric fencer reminded me of the times we got shocked while opening the wire gates that opened the way to the cows' pasture, and the barbed wire brought back memories of torn shirt sleeves, blue jeans, or work gloves.

In the morning hours, you could hear the hogs that used their snouts to lift the lids from their hog feeders and let the lids fall with a bang—as if trying to awaken us to let us know that the feeders were empty and that it was time to grind more feed. Those feeders and waterers were for sale.

As I recall, there was always a mineral block and a salt block in each of the cattle's hay bunks, and time and time again we'd carry bushel baskets of silage or bales of hay to the bunks for night feedings. The rusted but working welder came equipped with a face shield to protect the eyes from the brightness of the welding torch as it touched metal. We'd also use the shield to look at the sky on a bright, sunny day, or watch the solar eclipse—whether it was appropriate to use or not. Those were also some items on the auction bill that rekindled the past.

As this auction approached, there were some mixed emotions from family members. First there was the feeling of gladness felt for the parents who were at retirement age and would be allowed to enjoy other things in life without worrying about machinery breakdowns, sick livestock, and other woes associated with farming.

However, it was tough letting go of memories after living on the farm—so imagine how the parents felt after living there from their youth to retirement. It must have been hard on them when getting ready for the auction, removing the spider webs off the old antiques, filling hay racks with items that were small but nonetheless had their valuable uses.

That same machinery used by us when growing up and which we had cursed because of many a sore back or skinned knuckles while putting it together—most were stacked in several heaps of mangled scrap iron. Machinery that couldn't be fixed with different parts or by a weld were parked in a grove, but brought out for the public to see on sale day.

The auctioneers ran right through the list on the day of the sale, pointing and yelling a sale to the highest bidders throughout most of the morning and into the afternoon until nothing was left to sell. As all departed, it was a time of reflection and bewilderment at the next step, and what would happen to the farm and all its buildings once the land was sold and the former owners moved to the confines of the nearby city.

But not on that auction list, of course, were the priceless memories of growing up on that farm, of the holidays, the evening milking chores, the harvesting, the pride in knowing that while you owned the equipment, you also took pretty darn good care of the land that the farm thrived on. No one barked "Sold!" on that. That piece of satisfaction wasn't for sale.

For the parents and their family, it was time to move from one cow path to another, on to another phase of life.

Life moves on.

A view from atop the silo as the auction at the Hackenmiller farm commenced.

CPSIA information can be obtained at www.ICGtesting.com
Printed in the USA
LVOW060617060712

288993LV00001B/1/P